Randolph of Roanoke

*I would not live under King Numbers. I would not be his steward, nor make him my task-master. I would obey the principle of self-preservation, a principle we find even in the brute creation, in flying from this mischief.*

JOHN RANDOLPH OF ROANOKE
*at the Virginia Convention, 1829*

JOHN RANDOLPH

# Randolph of Roanoke

*A Study*
*in Conservative Thought*

By
Russell Kirk

The University of Chicago Press

THE UNIVERSITY OF CHICAGO PRESS, CHICAGO 37
Cambridge University Press, London, N.W. 1, England
W. J. Gage & Co., Limited, Toronto 2B, Canada

# *Acknowledgments*

TO THE several authors and publishers from whose books quotations are included in this volume, the author tenders his thanks for their kindness; and he is grateful also for permission to quote from manuscripts in the possession of the library of Duke University, the library of the University of North Carolina, the North Carolina State Department of Archives and History, and the Virginia State Library. The suggestions of Professor Charles Sydnor concerning the writing of this study were of great value; and Mr. W. C. McCann was so kind as to read the proofs.

RUSSELL KIRK

ST. ANDREWS, FIFE
SCOTLAND
May 1951

# Contents

## CHAPTER ONE

# Randolph and This Age

THIS little book is an account of the mind of a radical man who became the most eloquent of American conservative thinkers. John Randolph, the enemy of Jefferson, has been the subject of several biographies, one of them—William Cabell Bruce's—thorough and good. I do not propose to describe Randolph's life, therefore, but rather to outline his ideas and suggest their influence.

Randolph's career and character are familiar enough to those who read American history. His bitter hates and passionate loves, his fits of madness, his bewildering extemporaneous eloquence, his duels, his beautiful letters, his sardonic wit, his outbursts of prophecy and his visions of devils, his brandy and his opium, his lonely plantation life, his quixotic opposition to the great economic and political powers of his day—every one knows something of these. He was out of the pages of Byron and Disraeli. But he was also a man of genius, a genius literary and political. Few of us remember that he was a master of English style and a major influence in conservative social thought. A recent history of American literature, got up on a grand scale, has kind words for some obscure literary hacks but does not mention Randolph even in the Index; and he has not fared much better in histories of American political ideas. I think it is a pious act, pious in the old Roman sense, to call John Randolph up from among the shades.

America, which presently finds herself the chief protector of

the traditions of Western society and therefore a conservative
nation, has suffered from a paucity of men of conservative intellect. She needs to re-examine her first principles, if she is to
withstand the social atomization which most of the world is
experiencing. In consequence of this need, Calhoun's thought
already is receiving the attention it has long deserved. Randolph
was the preceptor of Calhoun, a champion of the old ways
when Calhoun himself was an innovator. But Randolph merits
study for his own sake. This volume is an analysis of his principles, dealt with topically, not chronologically. Our age could
profit immensely from a stricter study of Burke, and, in a
smaller way, we can benefit similarly from a reinvestigation of
the freedom-loving, innovation-hating Randolph.

John Randolph of Roanoke was born three years before the
adoption of the Declaration of Independence, and he died during the great nullification controversy. No man's life displays
more clearly the chain of events which linked the proclama-
tions of 1776 and of 1832. Jefferson, whose pupil, in a sense,
Randolph was, belonged to the earlier generation of natural-
rights thinkers; Calhoun, who, in a sense, was the disciple of
Randolph, belonged to the later generation which put its faith
in legal logic. Randolph sneered at both; he fought the administration of John Adams, and slashed the administration of Jefferson, and harried every other President of his time. In a study
of Randolph's ideas we can see the progress of the forces which
made inevitable the events of 1832 and 1861.

Yet Randolph's was not a philosophy of flux. Although
formed in an age of change, it was internally consistent. It was
an appeal to tradition, against the god Whirl, and it has its disciples yet. John Randolph battled the world of his day, and
three decades after his death his beloved country of Virginia
rendered to Randolph's principles the last full measure of devotion. His historical significance, both as influence and as index,
is great. Although Randolph and the other Old Republicans—

## Randolph and This Age

Nathaniel Macon, Spencer Roane, John Taylor of Caroline, Richard Stanford, and the rest—failed in their day to halt the political and economic march they dreaded, and at no time could command a majority in the nation or in the South, they were to triumph in the thirty years which preceded the Civil War. Randolph was to live to see the beginning of that victory, that fleeting triumph. No one would maintain that Randolph's impatient tongue alone caused this alteration in southern thought, but nevertheless Randolph exerted over the minds of the generation which followed his a force accorded to few parliamentary leaders. It was Randolph that Hayne quoted against Webster; it was Randolph to whom Calhoun listened, pondering, from his presiding chair in the Senate; it was Randolph of whom Beverley Tucker wrote to Hammond and his colleagues. The remnant of the Old Republican faction split during Jackson's administration: some, like Benjamin Watkins Leigh, became Whigs; some found their places among Calhoun's Democrats; some went over to the Jacksonians; some fought all parties. And yet a measure of the state-rights, aristocratic, libertarian, agrarian philosophy of John Randolph was retained by all of them, and those southern factions were to find themselves united in the year of Armageddon.

Concerning Old Republican political thought, little has been written. In recent years something has been made, with justice, of John Taylor of Caroline, an ally of Randolph's faction. Taylor's equalitarian principles, however, were by no means identical with those of Randolph. Randolph's speeches, which so astounded his contemporaries by virtue of their bitter wit, unpremeditated eloquence, and flashes of genius, never have been collected; nor have his numerous letters. We can read Taylor's and Thomas Cooper's and Calhoun's books today, but Randolph wrote nothing for publication except a few revisions of his longer speeches and a few letters to the newspapers. The man of Roanoke despised hard-and-fast expositions of political ideas and perhaps would not have written *Construction Construed* or *A Disquisition on Government* even had time and health permitted; in this, at least, he was like Jefferson.

In the following chapters I have quoted liberally from John Randolph's correspondence and addresses. I do not believe these quotations will be found tedious. I have let Randolph speak for himself because he was a much better writer than I can hope to be. And a chief purpose of this book is to make available a sampling of Randolph's work; as man of letters and as thinker, he is probably the most neglected of eminent Americans. Some of the passages quoted, often striking ones, have been printed nowhere else.

His thought was bold and cogent. The systematizing of his ideas is no easy task, for all that. Even critics like Henry Adams and William P. Trent, hostile to Randolph, concede that the Virginian possessed a remarkable—perhaps a unique—consistency in an age of political inconstancy. He would not bend before the demands of the hour, like Jefferson, wisely or not; nor would he alter his convictions, as Calhoun did with sincerity. From 1803 to 1833 his course was inflexible. It was not unchanging, however; he grew more intense in his beliefs and more bitter in the expression of them. The several chapters of this book are attempts to delineate the development of his ideas on a series of great topics.

Randolph was not a democrat, not a nationalist, not a liberal —as those terms are used today. (He did believe ardently in equality of civil rights, in his country, and in liberty, be it remembered.) Unlike Webster and Clay, he did not speak grandiloquently and sometimes emptily of the tremendous future of the Union. It may be that, right or wrong, he struggled against the stars in their courses. His principles surely are not in fashion in this world of ours. And yet Randolph's concepts of purity in politics and of personal and local liberty never can be invalid; even if for us they are as remote of attainment as are Plato's Ideas, yet they have the genuineness of Platonic images. Randolph's speech on Gregg's Resolution (March, 1806), concerning American foreign policy, never had greater significance than in these violent times; and his despair at the transience of social institutions never was better justified than in this reign of King Whirl. If our world will not accept Randolph's philosophy, at least we should have the hardihood to confute him.

## CHAPTER TWO

# The Education of a Republican

WHEN John Randolph was three years old, the Virginian legislature, influenced by Thomas Jefferson, abolished entail; in the same year, Virginia adopted her liberal constitution—a constitution far less democratic, however, than the reformed one Randolph was to denounce in 1829 (which latter document would be impossibly conservative today). When he was sixteen, he witnessed the inauguration of the new national government, "with poison under its wings." This revolutionary age won the youthful devotion of Randolph, but it did not fix him to the principle of perpetual revolution; indeed, he was to advocate watering the tree of liberty as infrequently as possible. Revolt against foreign dominion was one matter, revolt against old ways another. The Randolphs, Blands, and Tuckers, those great Virginian families with which John Randolph was connected, were American patriots, not Tories; reformers, not reactionaries. They were, nevertheless, American gentlefolk of the English pattern, great proprietors of Lower Virginia, lovers of liberty more than lovers of democracy. Randolph was to believe, in later years, that the abolition of entail was the death warrant of such families—as the new state constitution meant the rule of new classes, and as the federal government threatened the states with subordination. Yet his youth experienced the workings of these innovations only slowly, and the optimistic predictions of Jefferson could convince even the independent mind of John Randolph.

All Virginia was in debt to England in those days—tied, indeed, by many another bond, economic and cultural, to old England, bonds which Randolph, unlike his kinsman Jefferson, never desired to sever. Whatever the influence of obligations to the English upon the motives of the Revolutionists, the Virginian planters did not escape debt. Randolph himself complained not of the English creditors but of those in his family who had contracted the obligations; he lived in a two-room cabin and struggled with his nine thousand acres the whole of his life, until, just before his mission to Russia, he paid the last penny.

A Virginian planter did not allow his debts to alarm him overmuch, however, as Randolph was to complain of his order. Prodigality of a sort existed, but it did not infect Randolph; he was to oppose extravagance so sternly as to be charged with avarice. As for the other aspects of that Virginian life, they have been described often (in Beveridge's *Marshall,* for instance)— the rurality, the pride, the freedom coupled with Negro servility, the plantation houses that were great assembly rooms below and great barracks above. Henry Adams perhaps exaggerates the roughness of Randolph's Virginia,[1] but there were in it elements of license and folly. Still, not the nature of the life so much as the nature of the boy made the man and his political ideas.

Contemporary descriptions of this youthful Virginian suggest that Randolph was not likely to have been other than he became, even had he been born in another land or age. Perhaps it is true, as Parrington says,[2] that in no other country or time could such a man have had such a political career; but, even had he not been the fierce leader of the opposition, at heart Randolph could have been nothing but an implacable defender of his liberties and a critic of his era and his nation. One reads of his painfully sensitive body and mind, further irritated by the disease which seemed to dog all the Randolphs of his branch and by the eccentricity peculiar to the family; of his early intensity in love and hate; of his precocious genius. How could such a being ever develop into a democrat, ever sympathize with or endure the masses, ever lower his wit or his patience to their level? He was meant for a St. Michael, as his bitterest critic calls him,[3] and, when one remembers that with this nature he combined an inheritance and environment of pride and affluence, it seems amazing that such a man ever could become as much a popular power in politics as Randolph became, even in his day of a limited electoral franchise.

So it is that we should not attribute to Randolph's education any very great degree of influence upon his career. Even from infancy, he seems to have been unique John Randolph, with the sparkle and the torment of eccentricity. It seems probable that Randolph's reading, schooling, and experience of the world served chiefly to confirm and intensify the inclinations of his boyhood. Those deep-seated political prejudices which even the complacency of modern psychology has generally shied away from analyzing, those mysterious proclivities of character toward conservation or innovation, all tended in Randolph toward a veneration of the old order of things; and his solitary life, his perpetual sickness, and the probably consequent sexual impotence with which his enemies had the callousness to taunt him—these influences acerbated his temper and augmented his dislike of novelty.

*2*

Unlike his most formidable opponents in Congress—Webster, Clay, Calhoun—John Randolph came of a family possessing wealth and education. A library of respectable proportions was at his childhood home, "Matoax," near Petersburg. To his inheritance of great names was added that of the Tuckers, when, in 1788, his widowed mother married St. George Tucker,

poet, jurist, soldier, and statesman—and also the American edi-
tor of Blackstone's *Commentaries* and the writer of *A Dissertation on Slavery,* in which he attacked Negro bondage on the
grounds of natural right and economic expediency. This latter
book probably influenced Randolph's opposition to slavery;
and Tucker's edition of Blackstone was the bible of every Virginian lawyer. Tucker's annotations are a good exposition of
natural-rights doctrine. Although after Randolph's break with
the Judge, he sneered at the Blackstone, in his youth he appears
to have thought highly of it.[4] This was before he fell under the
influence of an immensely greater legal thinker, Burke.

Yet it was from his mother that Randolph received the direc-
tion of his reading and the greater part of his early education.
Doubtless he learned more from her, whom he loved with all
that passion which sometimes overmastered him, than from his
schoolmasters. A lady who knew her said of Frances Bland
Tucker: "She was a woman, not only of superior personal at-
tractions, but who excelled all others of her day in strength of
intellect, for which she was so justly celebrated."[5] Randolph,
long later, wrote of her: "Only one human being ever knew
me. *She* only knew me."[6] She nourished his oratorical talents:
"My mother once expressed a wish to me, that I might one day
or other be as great a speaker as Jerman Baker or Edmund
Randolph! That gave the bent to my disposition."[7] And it was
she, too, who told the boy, as they rode together over the red
fields, "Keep your land and your land will keep you."[8] The
lonely man of Roanoke never disobeyed that injunction and all
his life added field to field with an eagerness resembling
agrarian avarice.

Randolph suffered from a violent distaste for formal schooling—at no time in his proud life could he bear restraint—and
one notes his recurring denunciations of institutions of learning. This defiance of the powers that were, which ran all
through Randolph's career, became evident in his early years.
Ordinary schools were not for such as Randolph; as he said, he

"acquired all his knowledge from his library at Roanoke, and by intercourse with the world."[9]

What were the books of his early years? Randolph has listed many of them, particularly in his letters to Theodore Dudley and to his niece, Elizabeth Coalter. Best known is the letter of February 16, 1817, to Dudley, in which he praises *Orlando Furioso,* and adds:

> If from my life were to be taken the pleasure derived from that faculty, very little would remain. Shakspeare, and Milton, and Chaucer, and Spenser, and Plutarch, and the Arabian Nights' Entertainments, and Don Quixote, and Gil Blas, and Robinson Crusoe, and "the tale of Troy divine," have made up more than half of my worldly enjoyment. To these ought to be added Ovid's Metamorphoses, Ariosto, Dryden, Beaumont and Fletcher, Southern, Otway, Congreve, Pope's Rape and Eliosa, Sheridan, Addison, Young, Thomson, Gay, Goldsmith, Gray, Collins, Cowper, Byron, Aesop, La Fontaine, Voltaire, (Charles XII., Mahomed, and Zaire;) Rousseau, (Julie,) Schiller, Madame de Stael—but, above all, Burke.
>
> One of the first books I ever read was Voltaire's Charles XII.; about the same time, 1780–1, I read the Spectator; and used to steal away to the closet containing them. The letters from his correspondents were my favorites. I read Humphrey Clinker, also; that is Win's and Tabby's letters, with great delight, for I could spell at that age, pretty correctly. Reynard, the Fox, came next, I think; then tales of the Genii and Arabian Nights. This last, and Shakespeare, were my idols. I had read them with Don Quixote, Gil Blas, Quintus Curtius, Plutarch, Pope's Homer, Robinson Crusoe, Gulliver, Tom Jones, Orlando Furioso, and Thomson's Seasons, before I was eleven years; also, Goldsmith's Roman History, 2 vols., 8 vo., and an old history of Braddock's war. . . .[10]

Elsewhere, he mentions reading Xenophon, Demosthenes, Sallust, Cicero, Lucian, Virgil, Horace, Chatham, and Fox. He early became acquainted with other Greek and Roman classics and frequently commended them to his young relatives. He knew his Greek, Latin, and French, although he sneered at those who taught him. A brief and miserable attendance at Walker Maury's grammar school in Virginia, a year at Princeton, nearly two years at Columbia, and a few weeks at William and Mary constituted his regular schooling; it was his custom to depreciate his accomplishments at school. His complaints of these institutions were much like Jefferson's criticism of William and Mary College, and very probably academies and colleges were not for the precocious Randolph, recognized even by such gifted classmates as Littleton Waller Tazewell as the superior of his companions.[11]

For three years, 1790–93, Randolph nominally studied law under his uncle, Edmund Randolph, the attorney-general; the law was not for his impatient youth, and he thought his kinsman hardly a fit preceptor. On the flyleaf of his copy of Hume's *Treatise* he wrote: "This book was the first he put into my hands, telling me that he had planned a system of study for me and wished me to go through a course of metaphysical reasoning. After I returned the book, he gave me Shakspeare to read; then Beattie on *Truth*. After that Kames' *Elements of Criticism,* and fifthly Gillies' *History of Greece*. What an admirable system of study! What a complete course of metaphysics! Risum teneatis?"[12]

But what Randolph considered the insufficiency of his formal education was balanced by his private reading, some of which he later considered baneful. He found writers who deeply influenced the religious beliefs of his youth as well as the political faith of a lifetime. Writing, long afterward, to his intimate friend Brockenbrough, after he had turned from his former skepticism to devout Anglican belief, he stated that he had been

bred up in the school of Hobbes and Bayle, and Shaftesbury and Bolingbroke, and Hume and Voltaire and Gibbon; who have cultivated the skeptical philosophy of my vain-glorious boyhood—I might almost say childhood—hypocrisy and cant and fanaticism never fail to excite in men of education and refinement, superadded to our natural repugnance to Christianity. I am not, even now, insensible to this impression.[13]

When his house at Bizarre burned in 1813, he wrote, half-ironically, "I have lost a valuable collection of books. In it a whole body of infidelity, the Encyclopedia of Diderot and D'Alembert, Voltaire's works, seventy volumes, Rousseau, thirteen quartos, Hume, &c."[14]

A very different author, some biographers assert, exerted over the youthful Randolph an influence greater than that of any other writer: Edmund Burke. In later life Randolph mentioned Burke as foremost among his favorites. But when did the great Whig become his exemplar? One of Randolph's earlier biographers, Hugh Garland, insists repeatedly upon Burke's early influence, and another writer, J. G. Baldwin, contends that "very seasonably, Burke's pamphlet on the French Revolution came into his hands, and made a powerful, and, in the end, a controlling impression upon his mind."[15] Yet Beverley Tucker, Randolph's half-brother, in a review of Garland's *Life of Randolph,* demolished this hypothesis. John Randolph had indeed read the *Reflections* when it first appeared, Tucker remarked, but he considered Mackintosh's reply a masterly refutation. Randolph adopted the French calendar and used it almost until the end of the century. Though he was disgusted with Paine's coarseness, he admired his talents and dissented very little from Paine's opinions. Not until the latter four years of Jefferson's administration was Randolph

led to suspect that there may be something in the enjoyment of liberty, which soon disqualifies a people for that self-government, which is but another name for freedom. "It is ordained," said Burke, "in the eternal constitution of things, that men of intemperate minds cannot be free. Their passions form their fetters." We very much doubt whether Mr. Randolph ever had his mind awakened to this great truth until the time we speak of.[16]

Like Southey and Coleridge and Wordsworth, it appears, in Randolph an early generous enthusiasm for French visions gave way to a conversion to Burke's solemnly noble conservatism. One might draw a parallel between the courses of the brilliant British and American orators, were it not that Burke was happy (in some sense) in the hour of his death and that Randolph died when he thought his cause ruined.

So much, then, for the reading of Randolph's youth and its influence upon him. If we compare it with Jefferson's, we find Randolph more catholic in taste, except for scientific studies, in which the impatient Roanoke planter had small interest. We find it broader, too, than that of John Quincy Adams, as described in Adams' youthful letters. Randolph's fondness for the English novelists and dramatists is interesting—a taste extending, indeed, to the older English poets and to any book treating of English social life. We do not find this preference in the earnest Jefferson—Fielding and Smollett were not names frequent on his lips. Randolph seldom mentioned those juridical writers admired by Jefferson—no Kames, no Coke, though he must have examined their works during his legal studies. Nor is there evidence that he ever investigated, like Jefferson, Anglo-Saxon institutions; he cared nothing for what Henry Adams calls the futilities of *sac* and *soc*. In time Randolph was to refer caustically to Jefferson, with his historical approach to natural rights, as "the philosopher." Randolph read his Locke, of course, and Bolingbroke, Hobbes, and other English political writers; and though Randolph referred to these authors now and again, none of them seems to have affected his opinions profoundly. But boyhood education is not all, and it is worth while to glance at Randolph's reading during his maturity.

*3*

Some critics of Randolph's character have attempted to link Randolph with the Romantic movement in literature and to find some bond between literary nostalgia and southern political thought. A thorough survey of Randolph's reading defeats such an effort. The Virginian had, certainly, a lively interest in the writers of his day, but his admiration for the Romantics was strictly qualified, as his correspondence with Francis

Walker Gilmer, Brockenbrough, Francis Scott Key, and Josiah
Quincy shows. He admired Scott's best novels and condemned
his poorer productions; his preference for tales of British life
and tradition like *The Antiquary, Old Mortality,* and *Waverley*
contrasts strongly with his strictures upon Scott's medieval ro-
mances. He praised Byron's poetry but deplored Byron's character.[17] He announced his determination never to read the Lake
poets. Maria Edgeworth was his favorite contemporary novelist; this liking doubtless is evidence of his strong social interests,
for the parallel between landlordism in Ireland and in Virginia was strong, though in Virginia's favor, Randolph thought.
"I never could abide an Irish Tory."[18]

With the possible exception of Byron, Randolph's favorite
poet among his contemporaries was Thomas Moore, but he
liked Moore's satires, not his sentimental verses. "Tom Crib's
Memorial to Congress" delighted him. To Henry Middleton
Rutledge he wrote: "Tom you must know is my Aristophanes
—he stands next to Shakespeare."[19] The verses addressing the
American legislators as

> Most Holy, and High, and Legitimate *squad,*
> First *Swells* of the world, since *Bony's in quod,*

held no offense for Randolph, who replied to a critic of his oratory that congressmen should not be addressed as rational beings[20]—one of the many instances, by the way, in which his
repartee was inspired, unconsciously or (like Mirabeau's) deliberately, by his reading of Burke. That famous flaying of his
interruptors with the contemptuous ejaculation, "The little
dogs and all, . . . see, they bark at me," is drawn from *Lear,* of
course; but Burke had employed it in precisely similar circumstances in St. Stephen's.

No, Randolph was not an enthusiast for the Romantics. His
favorite authors were those quoted repeatedly by him in his
speeches and letters—Milton, Shakespeare, Cervantes, Fielding,
Smollett, Butler, Pope, Dryden, and Livy, to name a few. These

are not the tastes of "morbid sentimentalism," which charge
W. P. Trent brings against Randolph.[21] It is impossible to define in a single phrase Randolph's literary inclinations, particu-
larly since he lived in an age of literary transition. A prominent
Virginian thought Randolph's Roanoke library the best collection in Virginia, finding it deficient only in the sciences.[22]
Among the political works included in a manuscript list of
Randolph's books, one notes those of Aristotle, Machiavelli,
More, Sidney, Harrington, Hobbes, Grotius, Locke, Bolingbroke, Burke, Chatham, Blackstone, Day, John Taylor, and
lesser men, as well as a file of the *Anti-Jacobin Review*. Even
Randolph's enemy Richard Rush, who prefaced his pamphlet
satire on Randolph with the lines,

> The Fiend is long, and lean, and lank,
> And moves upon a spindle shank,

spoke of Randolph's great knowledge of books and of how his
conversations were filled with "sayings and mottoes from other
tongues and books—from the Whole Duty of Man, from Tom
Jones, Dr. Faustus, Shakespeare, Rochester, the Bible, Racine,
Pope, Sancho, Vicar of Wakefield, Virgil, Caleb Quotem, Patrick Henry, Juvenal, Jack Robinson, everybody; all this with
various additional infusions of classical, topographical, and
genealogical erudition, the genealogy comprehending man
and beast, king, peer, and race horse."[23]

A man of literary tastes so broad cannot be confined within
any corral of literary generalization. So far as we may draw
parallels with safety, we may say his tastes were in accord with
those of the old English gentleman, tempered by a vigorous
interest in contemporaries. "Thank God," he said, when he
came in sight of the English coast, "that I have lived to behold
the land of Shakespeare, of Milton, of my forefathers!"[24] Randolph condemned Fielding as a coarse and licentious writer—
"but his age deserved him." Still, it was to Fielding he turned
for an allusion which was to put a bullet from Clay's pistol

through Randolph's wrapper. The British mastiff quality in Smollett and Fielding summoned his admiration; the Gallic touch of Sterne—and yet Randolph, unwittingly, had something of that tinge—called forth his reproaches. In so far as he could make it so, his life was that of an English country gentleman; and his politics were those of a Rockingham Whig adapted to the Southside.

This was the education of the man who reflected in his speeches "a degree of classical culture that is without parallel in American parliamentary history."[25] In regard to Randolph's political thought, perhaps the most significant conclusion to be drawn from all this is that there was little of the radical to be discerned. Such might be the taste of a Virginian Republican, but it certainly was not that of a Jacobin. Whether the man determined the tastes or the tastes the man, here was no spirit of leveling, no love of innovation, no admiration of the *philosophes*—or, at least, such inclinations died early. One may find the influence of Puritanism and parliamentarianism but not the equalitarian spirit.

Randolph's literary opinions, like his political convictions, grew more pronounced as the years passed. If social radicalism ever should touch such a man, it could not cling to him long.

## CHAPTER THREE

# The Basis of Authority

OF ALL those vexed questions in what Coleridge called "the holy jungle of metaphysics," perhaps none has been more hotly debated than that concerning the basis for authority in government. Votaries of the monarch's divine right or of the people's natural prerogative, of Leviathan or of civil disobedience, of social contract or of law of sword, have waged the battle long, and its end is not yet. Although today many regular students of politics—including some given to scoffing at Bentham and Mill—have adopted the viewpoint of the utilitarians, the mass of people in this country, when they reflect at all upon such questions, probably adhere to a concept of natural-rights doctrine. But most writers and thinkers have abandoned the cause of Locke and of Jefferson (although perhaps we are living at the beginning of a revival of natural-rights principle) and maintain that, so far as natural obligation or divine injunction is concerned, we have but one natural political law:

> Because the good old rule
> Sufficeth them, the simple plan
> That they should take, who have the power,
> And they should keep who can.

Not that this state of society is impossible to modify by political order; but this rule of might, most modern thinkers seem to hold, is the only *natural* order. Society alone confers rights and privileges. This opinion is far removed from Lockian theory, and in England the abandonment of natural-rights doctrine commenced more than a century and a half ago.[1]

In America, however, the adoption of new systems of political thought lagged behind British speculation. Jefferson's theory of the rights of governments and men, so often discussed, depended upon a juristic concept of natural rights. John Dewey would have us believe that we need only substitute "moral right" for "natural right" in Jefferson's expressions, and we will have modernized Jefferson and made him, indeed, a sort of Deweyite;[2] but Jefferson often used the term "moral" in our sense and preferred to speak of *natural* rights. The juristic social-compact theory was reinforced in his system by the argument that American liberties were rights inherited from the free Anglo-Saxons, before the Norman Conquest, and never forfeited; as Gilbert Chinard writes, "The Jeffersonian philosophy was born under the sign of Hengist and Horsa, not of the Goddess Reason."[3] In John Adams' works we find elements of natural-rights theory; and although John Taylor of Caroline did not follow Jefferson strictly, he stated that there exist two natural rights: the right of conscience and the right of labor.[4] It is in the speeches of Randolph of Roanoke that we first encounter a thorough expression, in America, of opposition to the assumptions of the Declaration of Independence.[5] Randolph was not alone, it is true; by the time of the Virginia Convention of 1829, the new system of thought—or, perhaps, the revived old system of thought, long dormant—was strong in Lower Virginia and developing in power elsewhere; but Randolph was the ablest spokesman of this opposition.

To call Randolph "the American Burke" is no great exaggeration. Randolph's character was more like that of the elder Pitt, with "his intractable, incalculable nature, his genius tinged with madness."[6] But Burke's theory of indivisible sovereignty, his contempt for abstract harmony in government, his impatience with questions of legal "right," and his advocacy of "expediency tempered by prescription and tradition,"[7] accompanied by his reverence for the experience of mankind—all these were the principles of Randolph. The Virginian statesman did not share Burke's admiration for the party system and lacked Burke's veneration of the state; we see more of the Jeffersonian "necessary evil" spirit in Randolph. But Randolph agreed that it is the duty of an aristocracy, as Burke put it, "to enlighten and protect the weaker, the less knowing, and the less provided with the goods of fortune";[8] and Burke's cautious sounding the lead, his devotion to prudence, were also Randolph's. The influence of Burke's works upon the Virginian grew stronger as his experience of practical politics increased. An admirer of Randolph wrote, not long after the death of the Old Republican, concerning Burke and Randolph: "There is a volume of Burke now in the library of Congress, which contains copious notes in the handwriting of Mr. Randolph, evincing how closely he has studied and copied his great exemplar."[9]

Although Burke and Randolph might denounce the natural-right theories of Rousseau and evade the natural-right theories of Locke, they were not the men to deny that laws of nature exist—laws, that is, derived from the spiritual character of man and demonstrated in the pages of history. Liberty was no absolute and abstract "Right of Man," immutable and imprescriptible; but it was a privilege conferred upon men who obeyed the intent of God by placing a check upon will and appetite. As Burke's Tory friend Samuel Johnson appealed in the arts to Aristotelian nature, so ran the political appeal of Burke and Randolph—to human nature, to the ways of God toward man and civilized man toward man, and not to the romantic or historical concepts of irrevocable "natural rights." No "right," however natural it may seem, can exist unqualified in society. A man may have a right to self-defense; therefore, he may have a right to a sword; but if he is mad or wicked, and intends to do his neighbors harm, every dictate of prudence will tell us to disarm him. Rights have no being independent of circumstance and expediency.

Yet Bentham's materialistic view was as repugnant to Burke and Randolph as was Rousseau's etherealism. Although Randolph fought Jefferson's doctrines, his contemporaries spoke of him as a Republican and a liberal—a democrat, even. J. G. Baldwin settled this seeming paradox in a shrewd remark linking Burke and Randolph: "They were Whigs, in the ancient sense, because of their strong love of personal freedom—alone as deep and unconquerable as their pride; and because of their strong caste feelings; in other words, devotion to their own rights and to those of their order."[10]

Randolph was what Horace Gregory calls an "aristocratic libertarian."[11] His theory of the basis of authority was not one of those metaphysical abstractions he so despised but a deliberate defense of the old society he thought best and of the old state of which he was so fitting a representative. The unreasoning equalitarianism and idealism of Marryat's elder Mr. Easy would not do for him, and he fought with all the powers of his impatient logic the tide of the popular principles of equality and fraternity—and fought, too, that corruption of the principle of liberty which he considered libertinism.

None of the great Virginians were social radicals; as the Revolution in America was essentially a struggle for the preservation of old American ways, so were Jefferson's reforms aimed at the preservation of an agrarian society of freeholders—those freeholders whom Randolph, also, considered the strength of the commonwealth. The real innovators were not Henry and Jefferson and Taylor and Randolph but the westerners of Clay's American System and the Federalist manufacturers "north of the Patapsco." John Taylor assailed the capitalists not with the arguments of a modern Marxist, seeking to have the expropriated become the expropriators, but with the denunciations of an agriculturist who saw the doom of his society in the Bank of the United States and the tariff. But if the Virginians were not radicals, neither were they aristocrats, in the strict sense; their opposition to an established nobility—that is, to a small and special class maintained by law in the possession of exclusive economic and political privileges—was unrelenting. Nathaniel Macon, Randolph's colleague, once wrote to Van Buren: "Banks are the nobility of the country, they have exclusive privileges; & like all nobility, must be supported by the people & they are the worst kind, because they oppress secretly."[12]

Yet though Randolph denounced Toryism and privilege— unless one considers entail and primogeniture, the passing of which Randolph regretted, forms of privilege—he was willing to term himself an aristocrat, in the personal sense; one of the best of his epigrams is this: "I am an aristocrat; I love liberty, I hate equality."[13] No phrase more clearly reveals the gulf between the thought of Jefferson and the thought of Randolph.

Here, with respect to the question of authority, is the strongest proof of the power of Randolph's mind and of the influence of his oratory. Upon the question of slavery, the South went beyond Randolph and repudiated his opposition to the institution; in regard to his hatred of change, Virginia and the South and the nation were altered politically and economically, as decades passed, almost beyond recognition, for all his warnings; his ideal of inviolate state rights was doomed; and the agrarian society he loved has withered. Yet his theory of authority was accepted by the South of Calhoun and the South of Davis and is accepted—with little mention of Randolph—by many political thinkers today. His scorn for the Rights of Man and the Declaration of Independence, or, rather, for the literal and popular interpretation of those documents, has triumphed among the scholars over the idealism—an attractive enthusiasm, to be sure—of the days of American infancy. It was the devout Randolph who helped strike down the concept of equalitarian liberty as a divine gift; it was Randolph, the lover of old ways, who helped demolish the theory of a historical compact of freedom. Perhaps the man of Roanoke, were he able to look upon this success, would find small pleasure in it, for the society in the cause of which he denounced the principles of the Declaration was long since engulfed by our world; still, although in Pyrrhic fashion, Randolph has triumphed.

Little need be said of Randolph's opinions upon the question of sovereignty, since John Austin had not yet impressed that vexed question in all its ramifications upon political consciousness. Randolph was in substantial agreement with Burke, with John Taylor, and with Calhoun. Sovereignty rested in the people of a state; it was indivisible and not transferable; the true state was Virginia or Massachusetts, not the government at Washington; and, moreover, it was vested neither in a state government nor in a federal establishment but in the people themselves. Such was Randolph's premise when he found it necessary to discuss the matter. But his impatience with abstractions did not often allow him to consider the point in his speeches; for, like Taylor and many a man since, he considered the question idle. With Randolph, it was not so much of import where the abstraction "sovereignty" had been placed by process of law as of where it *should* rest—and where real power, which alone can maintain sovereignty, should rest. Randolph always aimed for the heart of things.

This chapter deals with the question of the origin of power in the state; with the question of who, and how many, should exercise the governance; and with the question of abstract rights against political expediency. Not until late in life did Randolph find it necessary to elucidate publicly his views on these topics; other matters were more pressing, and his disgust with government had not become so thorough. As an old man, disappointed in men and measures, he challenged the divinity of Demos— denied popular wisdom with that sort of boldness which had cost John Adams his popularity.

# The Basis of Authority

Whether in his early youth Randolph was a disciple of the philosophers of natural rights, it is not easy to say. He was a friend to France; he was an enemy to the "monocrats" and "aristocrats" of the Federalist party; and he was an adherent of Jefferson, although, as Adams is quick to point out, Randolph was no worshiper even then of the Monticello sage. But opposition to Washington and John Adams and Hamilton could be based more upon fear for the liberties of states and citizens, and distrust of the financial and commercial policies of the Federalist administration, than upon devotion to the abstractions of the Age of Reason; and, similarly, enthusiasm for the cause of France might be that sympathy with peoples struggling for independence which was Randolph's all his life rather than a love of Jacobinism. In his speech on Gregg's Resolution in 1806, less than a decade after he had been an advocate of the French cause, Randolph referred to those days:

Then every heart beat high with sympathy for France, for Republican France. I am not prepared to say with my friend from Pennsylvania that we were all ready to draw our swords in her cause, but I affirm that we were prepared to have gone great lengths. I am not ashamed to pay this compliment to the hearts of the American people even at the expense of their understandings. It was a noble and generous sentiment, which nations, like individuals, are never the worse for having felt. They were, I repeat it, ready to make great sacrifices for France. And why ready? Because she was fighting the battles of the human race against the combined enemies of their liberty; because she was performing the part which Great Britain now in fact sustains; forming the only bulwark against universal dominion.[14]

This left-handed tribute to the Gallomaniacs of the 1790's hardly has the ring of a man who ever held French principles; yet in 1797, Randolph, dating his letter "Floreal 10, 5 yr.," had written to Henry Middleton Rutledge a message sanguinary enough in tone to have satisfied Marat:

The friends of Freedom and Mankind are alarmed at the length to which the administration of this country have gone, but let not the emissaries & dependants of Pitt believe that any man or set of men can induce the free American people to embrue their hands in the blood of their Brethren. Before that period arrives I hope to see the advisers of such measures brought to the block: this is the only atonement which can be made by them for their political sins.[15]

Probably such expressions were only the words of a fiery youth who saw a free nation in its agony; for it is difficult to perceive any social radicalism in a letter to Nicholson, written three years later, in which Randolph stated, "I have a respect for all that is antique (with a few important exceptions)."[16] A few months afterward, he made some defense of Burr, then intriguing for the presidency, and found it necessary to add, "I am not a monarchist in any sense."[17] The Virginian planter could not long keep company with Gallic excesses; and, clearer of vision than many an English liberal, he saw Napoleon as a far greater threat to liberty than ever the Bourbons had been.

An early instance of his principle of basing governmental action rather upon "expediency tempered by prescription and tradition," than upon assertions of inviolable right, may be seen in a letter to Creed Taylor in 1802, in which Randolph opposed the creation of a separate state in western Virginia and regretted that the area west of the Blue Ridge was almost unrepresented in the Virginian legislature:

I am sorry that so large a portion as I have been told (23,000) was left unrepresented west of the ridge. I have not seen your new bill, but it would have been policy to have given them more than their proportion. ... It will forever fix the aversion of those oppressed people—for such they *now* are. Was it generous to crush an insect with the club of Hercules?[18]

In short, representation should be determined by the need for harmony of interests in the state, not by counting noses. As for direct representation, he had taken a similar stand in its favor earlier that year, when he had praised the character of the House of Representatives:

In this branch alone you will find the Republican character; in the other it is not to be seen. There, is that principle virtually acknowledged which gives to Old Sarum and Newton a representation equal to that of London; a principle which is believed by some essential to the existence of that well-ordered Government, or perhaps that of any other that they are willing to bestow upon man: the principle that the governors are not to be under the complete control of the governed; in other words, that the majority ought not to govern. In the appointment of the Executive the same spirit prevails, although somewhat modified.[19]

These statements prove what we have no reason to doubt—that during the greater part of Jefferson's first administration Randolph retained a measure of faith in the Jeffersonian democracy. But the break came soon; not on a question of political theory, however, but on one of political morality—the Florida question. Disgust with the policies of the Republican administration doubtless had its part in strengthening the conservative tendencies already to be seen in Randolph's course. By the latter part of 1805, he was sneering at Jefferson as the "political messiah"; scorning the reliance his fellow-congressmen placed upon authority as blundering "amongst a load of quotations from Grotius, and Puffendorf, and Lord knows who"; and exhorting them to be "not dreamers and soothsayers, but men of flesh."[20] They sought to base their actions upon "natural" principles; already Randolph found a different basis of authority. Soon Sloan, of New Jersey, who disliked Randolph for his reference to his proposals as "Sloan's Vegetable Specific," was comparing Randolph with Burke—invidiously, Sloan thought.[21] Randolph wrote to his ally, Nicholson: "Are you too denounced as a Jacobin republican? It seems there are two sorts coming into vogue, and I hear, (but do not see) that I am put down in that class."[22]

The "Jacobin Republicans," whose principles are discussed in another chapter, were anything but literal Jacobins; soon they were to become the "Tertium Quids," and Randolph never was to re-enter the Jeffersonian fold. His separation did not mean he would adopt Federalistic principles, as Jefferson expected;[23] in a letter of September 6, 1806, to his nephew, then in England, he praised the absence of established classes in America:

Here is no distinction of ranks; & here, most fortunately for you, the honest means, to which your want of fortune will require you to resort, to obtain an honest livelihood, will not cast you beneath any class of your countrymen ... much rather would I see you fixed to a work-bench, or following the plough, than leading a life of unprofitable and discreditable idleness. Active employment is essential to the happiness of man.[24]

But equality of opportunity did not mean equality of political privilege; he was at war with the growing demand for popular electoral suffrage. To Key, of Baltimore, he wrote, in 1813: "Electioneering is upon no very pleasant footing any where; but with you, where the 'base proletarian rout' are admitted to vote, it must be peculiarly irksome and repugnant to the feelings of a gentleman."[25] As in Fenimore Cooper, the characteristics of aristocrat and democrat mingled in Randolph. This was no inconsistency. For us, democracy has come to mean universal suffrage; but the people (a term susceptible of various definitions) may rule without "one man, one vote." For Randolph, the real people of a country were its substantial citizenry, its men of some property, its farmers and merchants and men of skill and learning; upon their shoulders rested a country's duties, and in their hands should repose its government.

There is no need to trace in detail Randolph's expressions concerning the basis of authority during the succeeding fifteen years, for it was not until 1822 that Randolph commenced a detailed exposition of his views. One finds, however, in his speeches and letters frequent condemnation of Jacobinism and unreality in politics, as when he wrote to Key in 1815: "England, I sometimes think, stands on the verge of some mighty convulsion.... Jacobinism has, I believe, a stronger hold in that country than in any other in Europe. But the foolishness of human wisdom, nothing daunted by the repeated overthrow of its plans, yet aspires to grasp and control the designs of the Almighty."[26] In a public letter addressed to a constituent that same year, he assailed the "air-built theories" of the national administration: "Anarchy is the chrysalis state of despotism; and to that state have the measures of this government long tended, amidst the professions, such as we have heard in France and seen the effects of, of Liberty, Equality, Fraternity."[27]

And equalitarianism, produced in part by Jefferson's radical alteration of the laws of descent, aroused his wrath; he wrote to Gilmer in 1821: "When our patriotic wise acres succeeded in breaking down the distinction between the gentleman and the blackguard, it was obvious that it would at length be effected by the extinction of the former class."[28]

A strong admiration for British institutions combined with events in America—the War of 1812, the elections of Madison and Monroe, the rise of the National Republicans, the decisions of Marshall's Court, the Bank, the debt, the tariff, and many another dose that was gall to Randolph—to prejudice him even more strongly against Jeffersonian theories. It was during the debate on the Apportionment Bill, in 1822, that the Virginian orator commenced his prolonged assault upon Jeffersonian natural-rights thought, Jeffersonian democratic polity, and Jeffersonian optimism.

⚘ *3* ⚘

A blow at the power of his Virginia launched Randolph against equalitarianism. The census of 1820 had shown the necessity of increasing the number of members in the House or of increasing, as an alternative, the size of the unit of representation; Virginia's population had not grown in proportion to that of the nation at large, and, were the unit of representation to be increased, Virginia would lose at least one representative. The indignant Randolph, foreseeing the eclipse of the Old Dominion by an industrialized North and a barbarous West, made a fierce stand for the honor and the rights of his state. There was no need for a fixed number of members in Congress, he insisted; it was far better to have a large House than to have congressional districts with a population so large as to sever the bond between people and representative. Here Randolph emphasized a principle he steadily maintained—that the legislator should be close to his constituents, from whom came his right to legislate. Randolph never yielded to the theory of virtual representation—that doctrine, best expressed by Mansfield during the pre-Revolutionary controversy, that lawmakers represent not a particular body of constituents but act for the people as a whole. In Randolph remained too much of the Revolutionary and Jeffersonian spirit for such an abandonment of local rights, even though the theory sometimes was gravely propounded on the floor of the House. During the debate on apportionment in January, 1822, he said:

Government, to be safe and to be free, must consist of representatives having a common interest and a common feeling with the represented. ... When I hear, said Mr. R., of settlements at the Council Bluffs, and of bills for taking possession of the mouth of the Columbia river, I turn—not a deaf ear, but an ear of a different sort, to the sad vaticinations of what is to happen in the length of time—believing, as I do, that no government extending from the Atlantic to the Pacific can be fit to govern me or those whom I represent. There is death in the pot, compound it how you will. No such government can exist, because it must want the common feeling and the common interest with the governed, which is indispensable to its existence.[29]

Randolph was right, after his fashion, for the representative federal government of his day was not the national, almost imperial, government that is ours. He would not have thought this government of ours "fit to govern" him. But though he held that a legislature must be truly representative, he added that a constitution-framing body, like the federal convention of 1787, need not represent particular constituents. "They were to present a wise and free constitution to our acceptance or rejection; to act not as an ordinary legislature, but as the Lycurgus, the Solon, the Alfred of the country.... It would be as competent for a single individual to produce such a constitution, as for any assembly of individuals—Mr. Locke's fatal and total failure to the contrary notwithstanding."[30] Franker, perhaps, than Burke, who to the last preserved an outward show of respect for Locke's concepts while undermining them, Randolph here defied the authority of the master of Rousseau and Jefferson and presently carried that dissent to greater lengths.

In Randolph's system small place existed for the social contract or for faith in collective popular political wisdom. And Randolph scoffed at the enthusiasts who, like Montalambert, demanded "absolute liberty":

But, the honorable gentleman has said, we are for lighting the candle of liberty at both ends. It is true, said Mr. R., that some of us do sometimes, for the entertainment of the House and the public, endeavor to serve up a roast Secretary, and get a sound basting for our pains. It is true, that the fat is sometimes thrown into the fire, and our own dinners gain nothing thereby. I hope, however, we shall not light the candle of liberty at both ends, or at either end; for, if we do, it must sooner or later burn out.[31]

Having thus disposed in his merciless way of an incautious adversary, Randolph proceeded to expose the follies of seeking abstract harmony in government, of expecting the great venerable Gothic edifice of society to conform to ideal classical proportions; with Burke, he believed that a state is better governed by the irregular patterns formed by common sense and tradition than by the laws of mathematics and the Procrustean methods of omnipotent majorities. The Constitution had not been designed with mathematical regularity, or upon abstract models, but was what later men were to call "a bundle of compromises." The very fact that small states count for as much as great states in the Senate; the equally obvious fact that the slave states possessed "black representatives"—men elected from districts in which, perhaps, slaves outnumbered freemen—these provisions revealed that the Constitution had been produced by practical statesmen, not by idealistic calculators:

It strikes me, said Mr. R., that we are pursuing theoretical principles, which ought never to have been permitted to find their way into this Government, to lengths from which eventually the most abstract and metaphysical must recoil; for, if they do not, in the madness of their projects and of their strength, they will pull down the House over their heads. We are pursuing them to a length subversive even of the principle of union. If any man raises against me the hue and cry of being an enemy to republicanism, I cannot help that; for, if my life will not speak for me, my tongue cannot. . . . How comes it that the State of Delaware has two members in the other House? . . .What does that right depend upon? Abstract theories? No, sir. Upon what, then, does it depend? Upon common sense—although no science, fairly worth the seven, and worth all the politics of any men who study politics in the closet instead of the busy haunts of men—of professors in a university turned statesmen.[32]

Gentlemen would reply, said Randolph, that such provisions in the Constitution were the consequence of compromise; they would be right; and compromise was what he recommended once more in this matter of congressional reapportionment— compromise, not a vain appeal to a misty "natural harmony."

In vain the Roanoke planter struggled against these forces of change; and, disgusted with the course of Congress, he sailed for Europe. Jacob Harvey, who accompanied him, was a Federalist and considered Randolph a representative of the democratic spirit, yet his anecdotes of the English tour show how Randolph's mind was inclining more and more toward a complete refutation of Jeffersonianism. Of Virginia, Randolph declared that "the days of her glory are past"—for with the repeal of the "good old English laws of primogeniture," the native Virginian aristocracy was supplanted by blackguards; and, in consequence, Virginia was losing her ascendancy in the national councils.[33] At a dinner in London

Randolph was questioned closely on American affairs, and amused them very much by his replies. He exposed what he termed the sad degeneracy of Old Virginia, and became quite pathetic, in mourning over the abolition of the laws of primogeniture. Some of the company thought this a strange complaint from a republican; and, before we separated, they really had nearly mistaken Randolph for an aristocrat!...I could not help telling Randolph that *I* was the best republican of the two, and I laughed at him for having played the aristocrat so well.[34]

Although Randolph possessed the talents of an actor to a remarkable degree, he needed no pretense to appear aristocratic in character, if not in politics. All the same, he was no Tory and criticized English institutions freely. "England is Elysium for the rich; Tartarus for the poor," he observed.[35] And of the ruinous English administration of Ireland, he told Harvey: "Alluding to the oppressions of both the Government and the Church, he said, 'The Lion and the Jackal have divided the spoils between them, sir; but if I had my way, I would "unmuzzle the ox which treadeth out the corn." ' "[36]

John Randolph would have scorned to set his course by any system of unalterable universals; like Burke, he saw no need for rigid adherence to a harmonious closet philosophy. Back in the United States, he told the House: "Whatever trespass... I may be guilty of upon the attention of the Committee, one thing I will promise them, and will faithfully perform my promise—I will dole out to them no political metaphysics. Sir, I unlearned metaphysics almost as early as Fontenelle, and he tells us, I think, it was at nine years old."[37] In the same debate he re-expressed his doctrine of the need for direct representation of constituents, which the concept of Congress as a kind of omniscient national organ threatened:

But, sir, how shall a man from Mackinaw, or the Yellow Stone river, respond to the sentiments of the people who live in New Hampshire? It is as great a mockery—a greater mockery than it was to talk to these colonies about their virtual representation in the British Parliament. I have no hesitation in saying that the liberties of the colonies were safer in the custody of the British Parliament than they will be in any portion of this country, if all the powers of the States, as well as those of the General Government, are devolved upon this House.[38]

Thus Randolph, again like Burke, combined a love of local liberties with a denial that they were a "natural" condition; they were bestowed by the wisdom of society.

Strict constructionist though Randolph was, he saw in a written constitution only an instrument and not the final source of authority or the final appeal from injustice. Men should obey a constitution strictly so long as it was endurable; but should the interpretation of it fall into partisan hands, or should a problem transcending the constitution arise, men must defend their liberties by other means—not their "natural liberties," perhaps, but that freedom which needs no historical or juristic sanction. The basis of authority, in short, rested upon the acquiescence of the citizen in the justice of the constitution, not upon the constitution itself. Jefferson would not have dissented from this doctrine; it was the question of inherent right to participate in the control of government, regardless of station, that was the crux of difference, although even on this point Jefferson altered his stand from time to time. Randolph first appealed to a right beyond constitutional guaranties in his speech on the tariff of 1824. It was many years later before most southerners lost faith in the safeguards of the Constitution, but Randolph despaired even then. He agreed with the Federalist Fisher Ames that "constitutions are but paper; society is the substratum of government." On April 15, 1824, Randolph said:

All policy is very suspicious, says an eminent statesman, that sacrifices the interest of any part of a community to the ideal good of the whole; and those governments only are tolerable, where, by the necessary contraction of the political machine, the interests of all the parts are obliged to be protected by it. . . . With all the fanatical and preposterous theories about the rights of man (the *theories,* not the rights themselves, I speak of), there is nothing but power that can restrain power. . . . I do not stop here, sir, to argue about the constitutionality of this bill; I consider the constitution a dead letter; I consider it to consist, at this time, of the power of the states; that is the constitution. You may entrench yourself in parchment to the teeth, says Lord Chatham, the sword will find its way to the vitals of the constitution. I have no faith in parchment, sir, I have no faith in the abracadabra of the constitution; I have no faith in it. . . . If, under a power to regulate trade, you draw the last drop of blood from our veins; if, *secundum artem,* you draw the last shilling from our pockets, what are the checks of the constitution to us? A fig for the constitution! When the scorpion's sting is probing us to the quick, shall we pause to chop logic? Shall we get some learned and cunning clerk to say whether the power to do this is to be found in the constitution, and then, if he, from whatever motive, shall maintain the affirmative, like the animal whose fleece forms so material a part of this bill, quietly lie down and be sheared?[39]

Randolph's "eminent statesman" here is Edmund Burke, of course; and the position of these two imaginative conservatives upon the "rights of man" is often misunderstood, as is their view of the origin of civil society. Proper constitutions, they both held, are the product of social experience; they are rooted in custom and prescription, which have a deeper validity than mere positive law. An abstract devotion to a written "constitution," Randolph is saying above, may be subversion of the actual constitution of a people, which depends upon traditional justice. Social compacts, whether alleged to have been made in the mists of antiquity or owing their creation to recent popular enactment, do not take precedence of the *real* rights of humanity which they profess to defend. Randolph joined Burke in denying the social compact as described by Rousseau and Paine. Like his preceptor, Randolph believed not that society is a contract in the ordinary sense of that word—no deliberate agreement of free individuals outside society, a historical and moral impossibility—but rather that society is a "contract" in the sense of a divinely ordained link between the dead, the living, and those yet unborn. As F. J. C. Hearnshaw observes, when "contract" is used in this sense, "language has obviously lost its ordinary meaning"; Rousseau and Paine are repudiated, and so is Locke's individualism.[40]

Similarly, Burke and Randolph denied the validity of the rights of man as erected into abstract absolutes by Paine and his fellows; they affirmed natural rights of a very different sort —natural rights in the Christian tradition, the moral view of politics which we may trace back to Hooker and Aquinas and the Stoics. Burke defines the *real* rights of men upon the classical predicate of justice, "to each his own." Men have a right to the benefits of civil society—to do justice, to the fruits of their industry, to inheritance, to the welfare of their offspring, to "instruction in life, and to consolation in death." But no rights to equality at the expense of others, no rights to political power regardless of ability and integrity, or to overthrow the traditions of society, can exist. These latter are parodies of rights, veiled vices.[41] Men's rights, in short, are not mysterious gifts deduced from a priori postulates; they are opportunities or advantages which the stability of a just society bestows upon its members. Paine and the French radicals and the American doctrinaires confused strong inclinations with abstract rights. *Wanting* prerogatives is not the same thing as possessing a right to them. These concepts are expressed repeatedly by John Randolph, sometimes by quotation from Burke, sometimes with the ardor of his own rhetoric.

Randolph's dissent from the principles of Jefferson, from *liberté, égalité, fraternité,* reached its climax two years later in his speech upon Negro slavery in South America. He mauled once more the enthusiasts for absolute liberty and then took an uncompromising stand against the doctrine of abstract natural rights, independent of circumstance and expediency. Randolph must be allowed to speak for himself at some length:

If, said Mr. R., I were, what I am not—an acute philologer—I should sometimes amuse myself with the manner in which words slip from their original meanings, and come to purport something very different from what any body ever attached to them when they first came into use; the word *sophist,* (a wise man), got so much into disrepute, that *philosopher,* (a lover of wisdom,) had to supply its place; the word *libertine* meant what a liberal means now; that is, a man attached to enlarged and free principles—a votary of liberty; but the libertines have made so ill an use of their principles, that the word has come, (even since the time of

# The Basis of Authority

Shakespeare,) to be taken in a bad sense; and *liberal* will share the same fate, I fear, if it contracts this black alliance. There are some other words, also, such as *principle, conscience,* which are also in great danger. . . .

But, sir, perhaps I may be told, that in case I do not accede to the proposition of the gentleman from South Carolina, the answer is very plain and triumphant to my resolution. That the principles of these South American States are the principles that were of high authority on another great question—the Missouri question—are the principles of the Declaration of Independence. What more will you have, what more can you ask? What resource have you now left? Sir, my only objection is, that these principles, pushed to their extreme consequences—that all men are born free and equal—I can never assent to, for the best of all reasons, because it is not true; and as I cannot agree to the intrinsic meaning of the word Congress, though sanctioned by the Constitution of the United States, so neither can I agree to a falsehood, and a most pernicious falsehood, even though I find it in the Declaration of Independence, which has been set up, on the Missouri and other questions, as paramount to the Constitution. I say pernicious falsehood—it must be, if true, self-evident; for it is incapable of demonstration; and there are thousands and thousands of them that mislead the great vulgar as well as the small. . . . There is another, which, taken from a different source, I shall speak of as I trust I shall always feel, with reverence—I mean faith without works, as the means of salvation. All these great positions, that men are born equally free, and faith without works, are in a certain sense, in which they are hardly ever received by the multitude, true; but in another sense, in which they are almost invariably received by nineteen out of twenty, they are false and pernicious. . . . In regard to this principle, that all are born free and equal, if there is an animal on earth to which it does not apply—that is not born free, it is man—he is born in a state of the most abject want, and a state of perfect helplessness and ignorance, which is the foundation of the connubial tie. . . . As to ignorance, Locke says that we bring no innate ideas with us into the world; it is true, but man is born with certain capacities—which assume the impression, that may be given by education and circumstances; but the mathematicians and the astronomers, who of all men on earth are the most unsafe, in affairs of government and life—who should say that all the soil in the world is equally rich, the first rate land in Kentucky and the Highlands of Scotland, because the superficial content of the acre is the same, would be just as right, as he who should maintain the absolute equality of man in virtue of his birth. The ricketty and scrofulous little wretch who first sees the light in a work-house, or in a brothel, and who feels the effects of alcohol before the effects of vital air, is not equal in any respect to the ruddy offspring of the honest yeoman; nay, I will go further, and say that a prince, provided he is no better born than royal blood will make him, is not equal to the healthy son of a peasant.[42]

Thus Senator Randolph, enjoying at the time a popularity to which he had long been a stranger and engaged in demolishing the policies of Henry Clay, disavowed a priori political deductions. Men are *not* born free and equal, in any sense commonly thought by the mass of Americans; theories of "natural right" are in fact contrary to nature; the Declaration of Independence is in part, at least, demagoguery. The immediate occasion of his invective was a threat to the southern institution of slavery; the ideas he enunciated had a broader application. Having ridiculed the concept of natural equality, in the same speech Randolph proceeded to attack infatuation with abstract harmony in government and the striving after impossible ideals of absolute liberty. These will-o'-the-wisp notions, he cried out, had led the United States to fantastic projects of interference in the affairs of South America and even Greece; these abstractions unrelated to political realities menaced the security of the South and the tranquillity of the nation. He quoted Burke upon abstraction as distinguished from principle—a distinction of considerable importance for the student of conservative ideas. "I never govern myself," Burke had said, "no rational man ever did govern himself, by abstractions and universals. I do not put abstract ideas wholly out of any question, because I well know that, under that name, I should dismiss principles; and that, without the guide of sound, well-understood principles, all reasoning in politics, as in everything else, would be only a confused jumble of particular details, without the means of drawing out any sort of theoretical or practical conclusion."

Randolph expatiates upon this theme. "If you want to know the effect of metaphysical madness, look to the history of the

French Revolution, and to the undoing of the country." That intellectual tendency which Burke and Randolph decry is best described by this epithet "metaphysical madness." Both conservatives regularly employed abstract concepts themselves, for both were eminently Christians, men of letters, and political moralists: religion, literary art, and disinterested politics cannot long subsist without the nourishment of general principles in some degree. Both believed in Providence, a divine origin of society, and a mystical bond between the generations of humanity—ideas which require as great a power of abstraction, if they are to be properly comprehended, as any man possesses. But Burke and Randolph detested presumptuous and pompous speculation upon those mysteries of human nature, society, and the cosmos which must end (because of the fallibility of human reason) either in a silly, delusory certitude or in nihilism. Still more did they contemn application of such "metaphysical madness" to practical concerns. We have remarked that Randolph and his master derided a priori political deductions; well, they also attacked certain a posteriori endeavors, the product of that speculative school which thought society could be reduced to inflexible operations determined by collection of evidence. Burke calls these latter doctrinaires "sophisters and calculators," and they were very nearly the counterparts of twentieth-century "social planners." They were the savants whom Napoleon and Destutt de Tracy (the first in contempt, the latter in commendation) called "ideologists," and they had their British and American disciples. When Burke and Randolph profess their disgust with "abstractions," then, they are speaking against two separate groups of innovators: the a priori thinkers, best exemplified by Rousseau and Hegel, and the a posteriori thinkers, like the Encyclopedists and Cabanis. Both schools assumed that society and human character could be reformed deliberately and universally through the enactment of their programs.

Against such presumption the common sense of Burke and Randolph, both of whom had a good deal of experience of the world in its practical aspects and both of whom adhered to the Stoic and Christian view of errant human nature, rose up indignantly. Like Canning, Randolph was deeply impressed by Burke's emphasis upon the virtue of prudence. Prudence is the foundation of all true statesmanship; in its political application, prudence is the application of principles to *particular circumstances*. Prudence dictates that men must not be treated as undifferentiated units, nor societies as mere aggregations of humanity subject to uniform causes and effects, nor the perplexities of politics as soluble by a few neat decrees. A professor may deal in general views unmodified by circumstances, but a statesman must consider the infinite combination of social facts —differences, for instance, between man and man, between society and society, in historical development, natural resources, religious tradition, intellectual attainments, local institutions, peculiarities of character. General moral principles do indeed apply throughout the world and to all men; but abstract political concepts, whether the product of a priori or a posteriori minds, cannot be applied abruptly and indiscriminately to that delicate growth called "society" and that sensitive moral being called "man." The political abstractions of both innovating schools were deficient in veneration, that characteristic so prominent in Burke and Randolph; they left out of account the fact that society is not a machine but a moral essence. Often the view of social nature which Burke bequeathed to modern thought is described, with questionable accuracy, as "organic." Burke and his heritors did indeed think of society as possessing a continuity like that of a living body; but their actual description of social continuity indicates that they had in mind more an immortality of spirit, much like that of the church, than a renewal of tissue. At any rate, the "sophisters and calculators" quite ignored the necessity for continuity, and for this Burke and Randolph drub them unmercifully.

Tocqueville repeatedly observes that democratic peoples insist upon simple ideas, capable of universal application; they are as intolerant of intellectual subtlety and qualification as they are of hierarchy. Randolph perceived with bitter clarity this marked characteristic of American opinion. It was wholly inconsonant with his own complex and mysterious nature, and he cut and slashed at it almost from instinct. Henry Clay, in so much a mirror of the American public, a kind of magnified popular opinion incarnate in a single politician, was the most conspicuous advocate of applying simple and unmodified American political concepts to enormous problems: the American System of industrial and territorial expansion and unification, the Panama Mission intended to express sympathy with simple democratic tendencies in Latin America and throughout the world—these measures of Clay's provoked from Randolph a flow of contemptuous, despairing invective reminiscent of Swift. Clay stood for the principle of simple uniformity; Randolph, for the principle of proliferating variety. Variety, private or social, great genius or mere eccentricity, is favored by an aristocratic milieu, Tocqueville writes; democratic ages demand conformity. Thus the future lay with Clay, but Randolph's warning against the perils of abstraction applied to reality and unitary concepts applied to complex questions have a significance enhanced by the agonies of the twentieth century.

Clay's Missouri Compromise had been the product of such democratic methods, an endeavor to gloss over a terrible problem by the application of a coat of generalities and a superficial reconciliation of interests; now, said Randolph, Clay and the body of opinion he represented were trying to extend visionary sympathies and solutions beyond the bounds of the United States by sending a minister to the congress at Panama. These vague schemes of social amelioration forwarded by President Adams and Secretary Clay would end in social destruction, after the French fashion:

> What was the consequence of this not stopping to parley with the imprescriptible rights of man, in the abstract? It is that they have now full leisure to meditate on the imprescriptible rights of their king in the

concrete: that is the result of devotedness to abstract policies—of their management—look at it in Hayti and everywhere—I would say, if I was not afraid of being considered as treating that subject too lightly, which lies heavy on my heart—look at the famous academy of Lagado, and you will have a pretty fair specimen of a country governed by mathematicians and star-gazers, from light-houses in the sky. It is mournful while ludicrous. I have seen men who could not write a book, or even spell this famous word Congress (they spelled it with a K) who had more practical sense and were more trustworthy, as statesmen or generals, than any mathematician, any naturalist, or any literati, under sun....

I must be permitted to say, that there exists, in the nature of man, *ab ove, ab origine,* of degraded and fallen man—for the first-born was a murderer—a disposition to escape from our own proper duties, to undertake the duties of somebody or anybody else.[43]

In the history of American political thought, only old John Adams equals Randolph in the virulence and penetration of his denunciation of "French liberty," grandiose notions that consummate in general misery; and, like Adams, Randolph perceived the fetters which must forever bind property to power. In this very speech on South American slavery, Randolph declared that the control of property and the possession of power are eternally wedded: "You cannot divorce property from power. You can only make them change hands." Fenimore Cooper was to say the same thing a dozen years later.[44]

After this manner Randolph of Roanoke, the friend of France in 1797, ended his congressional career as the relentless foe of the theories behind the French Revolution. He had been consistent. Randolph had proved himself a champion of liberty to the point of excess, although not of equality and fraternity; but his liberty, for all its occasional eccentric passion, was the liberty prescribed by tradition and delimited by expediency, not the absolute freedom of the *philosophes.*

John Randolph retired from Congress in 1828. His final, and perhaps most important, ideas upon the question of the basis of authority in government came the following year, when he was a delegate to the constitutional convention of Virginia. He went to Richmond to defend old ways against the equalitarianism of a melioristic age.

# The Basis of Authority

*4*

"I have lived and hope to die a *freeholder,* and when I lose that distinction I shall no longer have any reason to be proud of being your faithful servant."[45] With these frank sentiments, Randolph stalked into the Virginia Convention. Never was there another state constitutional convention like that of Virginia in 1829. Among the delegates were former Presidents, distinguished jurists, powerful legislators, and famous orators; and nowhere, except at the federal constitutional convention, perhaps, were the fundamentals of government more thoroughly discussed—the problems of right and power, of suffrage and office, of property and poverty, of permanence and change. The East stood against the West in Virginia; the old order defied the new; equalitarianism fought conservatism. The most frequent spokesmen of Lower Virginia were men like Benjamin Watkins Leigh, Littleton Waller Tazewell, and Philip P. Barbour; Randolph was silent all during the first period of the convention's sessions; but men waited to hear the orator of Roanoke, and at last he satisfied them. He defended everything old against everything new and completed his denial of the philosophy of Jefferson and of Paine. King Numbers, the fetish of equality, the passion for change, and the danger of abstract speculation all encountered the lash of his temper. "I go for blood," he had declared years before; and here he was savage in his detestation of tinkering in politics.

Thompson, of Amherst, one of the ablest delegates from western Virginia, listened to the speeches of Randolph and John Marshall and their allies with the alarm most Jeffersonians must have felt. Randolph and his party were declaring that "government has no principles," Thompson protested; they held that "the rights of man are a mere chimera, of distempered imaginations." No one, in the whole progress of the debate, had so much as mentioned Jefferson and Paine; once the name of Fox had been venerated and that of Burke execrated, "but now, Burke, Filmer, and Hobbes, judging from their arguments, have become the text books of our statesmen."[46]

Within bounds, this is a shrewd criticism of the philosophy expounded by Randolph at the convention. Randolph did not disavow principle, of course, nor did he approve the old Tories; but he reiterated his horror at "abstractions" in politics and cited the great authority of Burke. True natural rights, said Randolph, are imperiled always by the interposition of abstract rights of men; and so they were here at this very convention. It was proposed to set an age qualification of thirty years for election to the House of Delegates. Randolph espoused the cause of youthful politicians and ridiculed the insertion of such rigid provisions into a constitution. Expediency might hint, and public opinion insure, that very few young men should acquire much political influence; but it was unwise and unjust to exclude absolutely the whole class of young men, regardless of merit. "But, all this, I suppose, is in obedience to the all-prevailing principle, that *vox populi vox dei;* aye, sir, the all-prevailing principle, that Numbers and Numbers alone, are to regulate all things in political society, in the very teeth of those abstract rights of man, which constitute the only shadow of claim to exercise this monstrous tyranny."[47]

An assault on King Numbers, the monarch of the West, occupies the greater part of this speech of Randolph's—that question of the arbitrary power possessed by a majority over property and liberty which was later to attract the brooding intellect of Calhoun. Randolph continued:

Are we men? Met to consult about the affairs of men? Or are we, in truth, a Robinhood society? Discussing rights in the abstract? ... Do we forget, that we are living under a Constitution, which has shielded us for more than half a century ... ? To their monstrous claims of power, we plead this prescription; but then we are told, that *nullum tempus occurrit Regi*—King who? King Numbers. And they will not listen to a prescription of fifty-four years—a period greater, by four years, than would secure a title to the best estate in the Commonwealth, unsupported by any other shadow of right. Nay, sir, in this case, prescription operates *against* possession. They tell us, it is only a case of long-continued and, therefore, of aggravated injustice. They say to us, in words the most courteous and soft, (but I am not so soft as to swallow them,) "we shall be—we will be—we must be your masters, and you shall submit." To whom do they hold this language? To dependents? weak, unprotected, and incapable of defense? Or is it to the great tobacco-growing and slave-holding interest, and to every other interest on this side of the Ridge? "We are numbers, you have property." I am not so obtuse, as to require any further explanation on this head. . . . Mr. Chairman, since the days of the French Revolution, when the Duke of Orleans, who was the richest subject, not only in France, but in all Europe, lent himself to the *mountain* party in the Convention . . . so great a degree of infatuation, has not been shown by any individual, as the tobacco-grower, and slave-holder of Virginia, who shall lend his aid to rivet this yoke on the necks of his brethren, and on his own.[48]

Extortionate national tariffs had been imposed by a bare majority in Congress, Randolph reminded the convention; King Numbers will do the same, reckless of justice, whenever he is given his chance. Under the pretext of democracy, a bare majority of men, told by the head, will plunder the minority at pleasure; but it will be to their interest to keep the minority at "the highest point consistent with their subjugation" for the sake of the greater spoils.

Shall we, in Virginia, introduce this deadly principle into our own Government? and give power to a bare majority to tax us *ad libitum,* and that when the strongest temptation is at the same time held out to them, to do it? It is now a great while since I learned from the philosopher of Malmesbury, that a state of nature is a state of war; but if we sanction this principle, we shall prove that a state, not of nature, but of society, and of Constitutional Government, is a state of interminable war.

Then Randolph returned to his old assault upon "abstractions" as distinguished from principles; and even unmodified principles, applied indiscriminately, can do terrible harm. He subscribed wholly to the Bill of Rights, but the ideas it contained were intended for guides, not inflexible rules of procedure:

The Bill of Rights contains unmodified principles. The declarations it contains are our lights and guides, but when we come to apply these great principles, we must modify them for use; we must set limitations to their operation, and the enquiry is, *quosque?* How far? It is a question not of principle, but of degree. The very moment this immaculate principle of theirs is touched, it becomes what all principles are, materials in the hands of men of sense, to be applied in the welfare of the Commonwealth. It is not an incantation. It is no talisman. It is not witchcraft. It is not a torpedo to benumb us. If the naked principle of numbers only is to be followed, the requisites for the statesman fall far below what the gentleman from Spottsylvania rated them at. He needs not the four rules of arithmetic. No, sir, a negro boy with a knife and a tally-stick, is a statesman complete in this school.[49]

Subjection to King Numbers produces taxation without representation; for property will inevitably be exposed to the desires of the unpropertied. The theory that taxation is a voluntary grant for common welfare, which is expressed repeatedly by Burke, thus will be undone; taxation will become once more what it was under despotisms, an arbitrary assessment for the benefit of particular persons and classes. "I will put it in the power of no man or set of men who ever lived," cried Randolph in his piercing tones, "to tax me without my consent." Remember, he exhorted the convention, that property and power cannot be truly separated; if power be transferred to the propertyless, they will not remain long without property of some sort. Chief Justice Marshall, who sat there in the convention, had remarked that the power to tax is the power to destroy. The whole old order of society, the old commonwealth of Virginia, might be obliterated by this innovation. Just as man always had been in society, so man has always had an appetite for property, operating sometimes *per fas,* sometimes *per nefas.*

It is the first time in my life, that I ever heard of a Government, which was to divorce property from power. Yet, this is seriously and soberly proposed to us. Sir, I know it is practicable, but it can be done only by a violent divulsion, as in France—but the moment you have separated the two, that very moment property will go in search of power, and power in search of property. "Male and female created He them"; and the two sexes do not more certainly, nor by a more unerring law, gravitate to each other, than property and power. You can only cause them to change hands.

Levelers would say, he knew, that he was no "friend to the poor." But weakening the structure of society is no kindness to the poor. Look at the drunkard staggering from the whiskey shop, look at the slattern seeking him, and ask where are their children. You will be told the government has undertaken to educate them, and so provided for the idleness and the whiskey of the parents. "Among the strange notions which have been broached since I have been in the political theatre, there is one which has lately seized the minds of men, that all things must be done for them by the Government, and that they are to do nothing for themselves: the Government is not only to attend to the great concerns which are its province, but it must step in and ease individuals of their natural and moral obligations."[50] An admirer of Adam Smith and the classical school of political economy, Randolph feared the democratic power of positive legislation as a means of converting the economic system from one of private concern to one of public spoliation.

Rambling in this long and acid speech as was his fashion, toward the end of it Randolph returned to his original charge, the despotism of Numbers; and he pursued the topic throughout the remaining sessions of the Convention. It is unnecessary to trace the whole course of his remarks. He was the sternest foe of the "white basis men," who would give no representation to property; he appealed to the sons of freeholders, not yet freeholders themselves, to stand by the old constitution. Only the owners of land, said Randolph, were fit to decide the policies of the commonwealth. He denounced all "tinkering" with government. He scoffed at the theories of Jefferson, never meant for practical men: "Sir, if there be any point in which the authority of Mr. Jefferson might be considered as valid, it is in the mechanism of a plow." For Mr. Jefferson had designed and sent to the savants, at Paris, a model plow, exhibited in the Jardin des Plantes. It was mightily admired by the savants; but when applied to the red Virginia clay, in competition with the ill-looking Carey plow, it was beaten as thoroughly "as common sense will always beat theory and reveries. . . . So much for authority!"[51]

The innovators did not realize half the mischief they were doing, he exclaimed; they were establishing a monstrous government, with two branches of the legislature representing the very same voters, pitted against each other until one should submit—the whole profound idea of representative government as a harmonizing of separate interests thus forgotten. "A Government of numbers in opposition to property was Jacobinism, rank Jacobinism."[52] Society thus roughly handled ceases to be a concord and is transformed into malignant factions—all this in the name of reform. Randolph's view is succinctly put by a passing observation of George Santayana's: "A reformer hewing so near to the tree's root never knows how much he may be felling."[53]

Legislators must be the representatives of small constituencies, of distinct local interests, or they fail to reach their proper function, Randolph continued; but, once chosen, a representative must be permitted to exercise his own virtue and knowledge: "He thought the people were trustworthy—just so far as this—they were very capable of choosing their own agents. They had sagacity and virtue enough to decide between worth and wisdom and intelligence on the one side, and their opposites on the other; and they having established their agents with power to act for them, he was for leaving more to those agents than some gentlemen seemed willing to do."[54] On the last day of the convention, once more he praised true representative government and denounced fulsome flattery of the people, who can act safely only through agents. Once he had been thought an overviolent Republican, he knew, but now the innovators had left him far behind, "thought an Aristocrat by those whom I think ultra Jacobins." Like the uninformed owner of a plantation, the people can be secure only if they obtain the services of honest overseers rather than undertaking the conduct of affairs themselves: "Yet they may be lured to their destruction by elections in November, and elections in April ... when they are called to pass upon an act of Assembly, containing thirty or forty sections—of which one-tenth—no, sir, not one-tenth—even of the Assembly that passed it—know the true meaning."[55]

The legislative initiative, the recall, direct primaries, and those other instruments of popular power which have grown up since Randolph's time would have met no warmer welcome from him than did this variety of the referendum; and no doubt he would have loathed the political consequences of these devices, though he might have been surprised that government still can function at all, despite such excrescences.

Marshall, Randolph, and the other leaders from the eastern counties succeeded in modifying the proposals of the western delegates, but they could not prevent the adoption of the new constitution, for which Lower Virginia voted in the fear that, if it should be rejected, a worse might be framed. Even Randolph was forced to yield after this fashion; and a year later he wrote to President Jackson (rather a curious confidant on such a topic) in terms quite as bitter as those of Sir Walter Scott after the Reform Bill which passed Parliament in 1833. Abolishing the freehold franchise had thrown government into the hands of the scum of the country; referring to the route from Roanoke to Charlotte Court House, he declared: "On the whole road there is not one person who can read or write and hardly one that is not a sot or notorious receiver of stolen goods, from slaves instigated to steal by the wretched 'House Keepers' who by the votes of Fenton Mercer and Madison and Monroe! were made voters at our elections by our new Constitution."[56] Randolph's "people," the farmers and men of substance, had given way to poor white trash.

J. R. Cooke, of Frederick, one of the "white basis men" who had thus succeeded in forcing the adoption of a general suffrage, expressed his astonishment, now the convention was done, that Randolph and his Tidewater colleagues had repudiated the doctrines of Locke and, infatuated with their own brilliance, had contended that there are no original principles of government; that natural freedom and equality are mere abstractions; that the doctrine of majority rule is "a vulgar fallacy"; that a government of numbers is legalized rapine; that the distribution of political power must be decided by "an enlarged expediency," without reference to natural rights.[57] Though Cooke somewhat misstated Randolph's position upon two of these points, it certainly was perfectly true that by 1830 Randolph had severed completely any ties to Locke, Paine, and Jefferson. In the last year of his life he wrote: "I cannot live in this miserable, undone country, where, as the Turks follow their sacred standard, which is a pair of Mahomet's green breeches, we are governed by the old red breeches of that Prince of Projectors, St. Thomas of Can*ting*bury; and surely Becket himself never had more pilgrims at his shrine than the saint of Monticello."[58] The old families of Virginia, he predicted, would sink into the mass of overseers' progeny, extinguishing the aristocracy of blood which Randolph prized as highly as any peer: "And this is the legitimate, nay, inevitable conclusion to which Mr. Jefferson and his levelling system have brought us."[59]

≈ 5 ≈

"I was not born to endure a master," Randolph wrote.[60] He might have added that he was not born to endure many equals; his impatient genius could not bear the failings of other men, nor could it descend to demagoguery. Had the basis of the franchise been earlier what it became in 1830, probably Randolph could not have gained office, for the distinction of "freeholder" upon which he prided himself also provided the only kind of constituency which would have tolerated Randolph's course as a political free lance. Tocqueville remarks the dislike of democratic peoples for eccentricity, and only Southside Virginia, perhaps, retained sufficient of the ancient aristocratic temper to elect so startling a man to high responsibility as late as 1828. Natural liberty, equality, and fraternity were ideas congenitally foreign to such a character as Randolph's, especially when a mind of his temper was joined to the possession of great estates and hundreds of slaves. Jefferson remained constant to these equalitarian principles, but Jefferson had little of Randolph's intolerant hauteur.

Far more than temperament, all the same, lay behind Randolph's dissent from Revolutionary principles. He saw clearly to what conclusions such ideas led and to what limbo they would consign the old life he loved. Whether his society or ours be the better, he was a true prophet, for the America of his time has been obliterated; perhaps he was wiser than Jefferson, since a change of this description was more than Jefferson bargained for.

Randolph found the source of authority not in a mystic Nature but fundamentally in force—force tempered by the experience of man and softened by the wise conventions of society. With Aristotle, he believed that man out of society must be either a beast or a god; there never had been a condition of truly human existence which was not a state of society. The real and ineradicable sources of political power are vigor of mind and body, possession of property. Equality and fraternity, far from being natural rights, are artificial conventions, to be extended or contracted as the requirements of a particular society dictate. As for liberty, individual and national freedom, although it was not an abstract right of man, it was a natural objective, a longing inherent in the character of men; and the Roanoke statesman never denied its blessings, although the exigencies of society might require that in particular cases liberty be restrained. "Art is man's nature," Burke had said; and Randolph, never forgetting this precept, declared that the art of politics consists in a prudent conformity of practice to principle, not in a fanatic devotion to abstraction.

Nothing of the leveler endured in Randolph, but he, like John Taylor, held that government should not deliberately produce inequality through legislation.[61] An aristocracy of this sort he roundly condemned: "Must we, too, have these Corinthian ornaments of society because those countries have given in to them?"[62] But men should not vainly endeavor to use the power of the state for equalizing natural distinctions, either; that, Randolph said, would be bleeding a healthy animal to aid a sick creature. Randolph dreaded the power of positive law, controlled by democracies, to sweep away the variety and liberty of life.

Real freedom and proper station in society must be determined by a noble expediency, guided by traditional moral principle. Fundamental principles of government can be discerned; individual liberty is one of them; but such principles admit exceptions—they are not legislative enactments. Ordinarily Randolph assailed the theories expressed in the Declaration of Independence "in the sense in which they are commonly understood by the multitude"; he did not wish to be thought an enemy to equality of civil rights, the sensible meaning to be got from the assertion that "all men are created free and equal." Equality before the law had no more determined advocate than Randolph, but there was no stronger opponent of political and economic leveling. Justice and democracy are not synonymous; courage and vigilance are required to keep them even compatible. It is no paradox that a government professedly equalitarian, like that of Cleon or that of the Soviets, can be arbitrary as a government professedly autocratic, like that of Critias or that of Spain. Randolph's warning that enfranchisement does not bring tranquillity needs recalling.

If, then, men cannot enjoy equal political and economic status, the degree of popular participation in government should be decided by enlightened expediency. Power and property cannot be separated permanently, said Randolph; and, if they change hands, usually it is with a disastrous interlude. Power, therefore, should be in the trust of men of property, landed property—freeholders, the strength of the commonwealth, qualified by interest and ability to comprehend the nature of government. They need not be the Federalists' "rich and well-born"; they need only be sturdy farmers and planters. It is to their interest that government be just; they, the pride of any state, are deserving of this prerogative; and they are numerous enough to maintain government. Perhaps Randolph's system never could have endured, whatever the course of national events, for the equalitarian spirit was immensely strong, and in industrial America (which would have been anathema to Randolph) freeholders are not more than a small proportion of the population. At any rate, the tariff, the rise of capitalism on a vast scale, and the decay of Virginian agriculture quashed the society of Jefferson and Randolph.

As Randolph declared during his famous denunciation of the "corrupt bargain" of J. Q. Adams and Clay, the "Blifil and Black George" speech, he was, in his day, "beaten down, horse, foot, and dragoons!" But his political ideas were to attain a fleeting triumph in the South. Fifteen years after Randolph's death, Calhoun was to write concerning natural-rights doctrine, specifically acknowledging the influence of Randolph:

> We now begin to experience the danger of admitting so great an error to have a place in the declaration of our independence. For a long time it lay dormant; but in the process of time it began to germinate, and produce its poisonous fruits.... Instead, then, of all men having the same right to liberty and equality, as is claimed by those who hold that they are all born free and equal, liberty is the noble and highest reward bestowed on mental and moral development, combined with favorable circumstances.[63]

In Calhoun, whom he distrusted, Randolph found his disciple; and in the minds of the political metaphysicians, whom he despised, he found his victory.

( 51 )

## CHAPTER FOUR

# The Division of Power

IN 1813 John Randolph, the bitter opponent of a war that had been popular in its inception, told a hostile Congress and a hostile people who were accustomed to his acerbity:

I have said, on a former occasion, and if I were Philip, I would employ a man to say it every day, that the people of this country, if ever they lose their liberties, will do it by sacrificing some great principle of free government to temporary passion. There are certain great principles, which if they be not held inviolate, at all seasons, our liberty is gone. If we give them up, it is perfectly immaterial what is the character of our Sovereign; whether he be King or President, elective or hereditary—it is perfectly immaterial what is his character—we shall be slaves—it is not an elective government which will preserve us.[1]

This was Randolph's exhortation to the nation—commonly an unheeding nation—throughout his fiery career: a demand for government of law and precedent, not of men and enthusiasm; for a known and unbending delimitation and balancing of the governing power, not the constitutional construction of opportunism; for a maintenance of the principles of freedom, whatever their passing inconvenience, and not a grasping at temporary benefits, whatever their ultimate consequence. Randolph was a strict-constructionist, a state-rights man, a jailer of that necessary evil, government; he fought the Federalists, the imperialists, the latitudinarians, the centralists, the "energymen," and, if they often forced him to give ground, still he held them back from the keep of his Old Republican castle and maintained the fight until a later generation took up the battle.

## The Division of Power

The state-rights, strict-construction views Randolph held were in no sense peculiar to him, of course; they were the tenets of all the Virginians of his school and of many men throughout the Union, particularly in the seaboard states of the South; but his constituents of Charlotte County called him, with truth, in a resolution passed after his death, "the most intelligent, the most consistent, and the most intrepid, advocate of the Rights and Sovereignty of the States."[2] John Taylor of Caroline held the pen of the Old Republican faction—a rather unwieldy pen, perhaps, although Taylor's style has been too harshly criticized, in part because of Randolph's complaint that Taylor needed a translator for his books—but Randolph was the orator of the cause, and his tongue was as dexterous as Taylor's pen was ponderous. Other men maintained these doctrines; but none defended them more ably, clung to them more inveterately, or impressed them more thoroughly upon the minds of the younger generation of political leaders. Now, nearly a century and a half since Randolph commenced his political career, these issues of state prerogative and constitutional construction are debated with scarcely less heat than in his day. Let us look at some of his more important declarations on these questions— still acid, still lucid.

The great object of Randolph and the Old Republicans, in a political sense, was the restriction of the power of government to that sphere specifically assigned by constitution and precedent. They admitted that at times such a jealous interpretation might lead to a passing difficulty; they conceded that temporary benefits might sometimes be got by exceeding the letter and spirit of the law. But, they declared, these annoyances or restrictions must be endured if free government and constitutional rights are to be maintained. The Old Republicans, respecters of precedent, perceived how dangerous and how irresistible a force is faulty precedent; the exception becomes the rule, war powers become peace powers, and, if a stand ever is to be made, it must be at the outset. Once the dike of constitutional guaranties is out, innovation pours through without interruption. The stern reluctance of the Old Republicans to allow government one jot more power than was specifically granted seemed a splitting of hairs to many of their contemporaries, and certainly seems so to most men today; but often the question with the Old Republicans was not the problem immediately at stake but the far vaster principle of the rule of law. It was upon this point of rigid construction of the federal compact, this insistence that principles are not to be abandoned no matter how tempting the prospect opened by making exceptions, that Randolph must have separated from the party of Jefferson even had there been no Yazoo debate, no Florida affair, no embargo; for those issues passed away, and Randolph was not reconciled to the Jeffersonian body; the difference was more fundamental. Whether or not Randolph was correct, historically and philosophically, it still is noteworthy that the three Presidents whose straying from the principles of republicanism he so condemned did not deny his premises; they, too, agreed that the Constitution must be construed strictly; but they, once in office, began to sacrifice construction to the demands of the hour, rightly or wrongly. Power corrupts, said Randolph. The time was to come when all three—Jefferson, Madison, and Monroe—were to lament the pass to which loose construction had brought the nation and were to return to the faith which Randolph never had abandoned.

A discussion of Randolph's thought on the subject of the division of power must embrace a number of subjects: the construction of the Constitution; the rights of states and the nature of the Union; limitations upon authority, by whomever exercised; and the struggle between sections. As Randolph's life neared its end, that question of the division of power became the problem of the hour in the form of the ominous nullification controversy.

It may seem strange that one aspect of the question is not discussed, except incidentally, in this chapter—the problem of sovereignty. It is omitted because Randolph omitted it, with his impatience of abstractions. He understood the problem, and, like John Taylor, considered it vain; while Taylor undertook the trouble of proving that sovereignty was indivisible and irremovable from the people of the separate states, Randolph only made this explanation implicit in his speeches. "Asking one of the States to surrender part of her sovereignty is like asking a lady to surrender part of her chastity," said Randolph.[3] For him, there was no half-mystic body of sovereignty, divisible or indivisible; there was only the question of how men best could govern themselves, as experience and their circumstances permitted. He was willing to allow the metaphysicians to place sovereignty where they willed, so long as power itself remained properly allotted.

*2*

Whatever charges hostile critics of Randolph may bring against him, they cannot deny his early and enduring devotion to the principle of strict construction of the Constitution, although they may attempt to prove his defense of the constitutionality of the Lousiana Purchase a momentary wandering from that narrow path. Randolph's whole congressional career is a record of protest against measures on the ground of their unconstitutionality, whether or not he favored their ends. Equally constant was his advocacy of the rights of the states. In 1802 he insisted that representatives were the delegates of the states in their respective individual capacities, not of the people of the United States at large, or as a nation: this was a deliberate distortion of the plain intent of the men who made the Constitution, Randolph pointed out, for, if such had been the intent of the convention, representation in the House would have been allotted by federal districts, without regard for state lines. Make such assumptions, and you destroy the federal character of government.

Another of his early speeches on the question of federal power against state sovereignty was delivered in 1805; it concerned the proposed exemption of colleges from the duties imposed in the tariff schedule. Randolph spoke against this bill and, at some length, dealt with the limited powers of the federal government and with the need for uniformity of legislation and the danger of special concessions and discriminations; he told of the importance of strict constitutional construction and of previous false construction, the work of his great fellow-Virginian, friend, and political adversary, John Marshall.[4] Not long afterward, during the debate on "preservation of the peace," he asserted the right of a state to serve processes in federal territory and the concurrent jurisdiction of the state with the national authority over coastal waters—a question still perplexed.[5] The doctrines of strict construction and of state rights even then were inseparably joined in his mind, and their union became more important as the years passed. These were the doctrines of the Republican party—or had been the doctrines of that party before it had attained power; yet, even in Jefferson's first term of office, Randolph found Republicans who opposed him, by word or implication, and the time was not long before he discovered himself, with his adherence to old principles, in the minority. For President Jefferson, too, was leaning—or was being forced to lean, by circumstances—toward interpretations of power more federalistic and latitudinarian than Republican. Some biographers defend Jefferson's vacillations on the ground that they only show that the man of Monticello was not slavishly devoted to abstract principles; but Jefferson was to regret the consequences of cutting the dikes of strict construction, precisely as Randolph, much sooner, came to regret the Louisiana Purchase. Many of the Republicans of the North were only superficially strict-construction men and champions of state rights, and, as Henry Adams points out repeatedly in his history of Jefferson's administration, it was upon them that Jefferson came to depend for his most constant support—upon devoted followers like Smilie of Pennsylvania and Sloan of New Jersey, legislators of a type far different from Randolph. The satirist Hugh Brackenridge sneered at the northern democrats in Congress and called election to that body "a stain worse than stealing sheep";[6] at all events, they were more equalitarian democrats and personal followers of Jefferson than they were adherents to the famous Virginian school of thought, and it is not surprising that Randolph soon parted company with them. As early as 1801, he was writing of these doubtful allies:

Parties here consist of the old Federalists courting popularity—these are a small minority; the same kind of characters, Republicanized, and lukewarm Republicans, who added to the former, will perhaps constitute a bare majority of the House, and Republicans who hold the same principles now that they professed under adverse fortune, and who, *if they were all here,* might amount to about 50 members. These are determined to pay the debt off, to repeal the internal taxes, to retrench every unnecessary expense, military, naval, and civil, to enforce economy as well upon men calling themselves Republicans as upon Federalists, and to punish delinquents without respect to their political professions.[7]

Four years later, Randolph was to find his band of what he considered true republicans reduced to half the fifty he had numbered in 1801; and, after Jefferson had left office, he was to say of that President's administration:

It had my hearty approbation for one-half of its career. As to my opinion of the remainder of it, it has been no secret. The lean kine of Pharaoh devoured the fat kine. The last four years, with the embargo in their train, ate up the rich harvest of the first four, and, if we had not some Joseph to step in, and change the state of things, what would have been now the condition of the country? I repeat it: never has there been any administration which went out of office and left the country in a state so deplorable and calamitous as the last.[8]

Randolph of Roanoke often was to refer in nostalgic fashion, in later years, to the first administration of Thomas Jefferson, with all its reforms. Indeed, there was not one adminstration after that time to which Randolph gave his continued support, although, had he lived until the succession of Tyler, he might have approved of the policies of that Virginian President; but by Tyler's time it was too late to turn back the course of events to Old Republican ways, and if the South Carolina school, and many leaders in other states of the South, later adopted the principles of the Old Republicans, still they remained a national minority and finally were crushed by force. The triumph of Randolph's republicanism—of anti-federalism—was brief indeed; but enough of that spirit survived after 1804 to feed a flame which is not yet wholly out.

> I confess that I have (and I am not at all ashamed to own it) an hereditary attachment to the state which gave me birth. I shall act upon it as long as I act on this floor, or anywhere else. I shall feel it when I am no longer capable of action anywhere. . . . I recollect an old motto, that always occurs to me at the approach of every thing in the shape of an attack upon my country—it is, *Nemo me impune lacessit.*[9]

This passion for personal and local liberties meant a distrust not only of national authority and congressional tinkering but of the executive branch, the judiciary, and, within the states, of the state governments themselves. Randolph sometimes repeated, "This is a government of suspicion, not of confidence"; and his suspicion, certainly, never slumbered. He was ever alert to denounce executive usurpation of authority, to deny the power of the Supreme Court to define the Constitution, and to check the inclinaton of Congress for legislating. Even concerning government in his own Virginia, he spoke of "the puzzle of state politics," of pettiness and corruption. Closely linked with these problems of the division of power is the problem of constitutional construction. A great part of Randolph's life was spent in demonstrating that American state and private liberties are dependent upon a rigorous interpretation of the Constitution.

It often has been asserted that the strict-construction men interpreted the Constitution strictly only when their interests were threatened by a loose interpretation; and it also has been held that state rights were asserted only when a state found involved some immediate interest. These contentions cannot be maintained in the case of John Randolph. Many a southerner of a later day, many a defender of slavery, held that Congress had no exclusive right of government over the territories; but Randolph, southerner and defender of slaveholding against northern assaults, still maintained that Congress governed the territories—and the District of Columbia, too—absolutely, as an empire. This was, undeniably, a proof of the penetration of his thought; for if he had said, as many did, that Congress was compelled to govern the territories in the "spirit" of the Constitution, he would have admitted that there was a "spirit," presumably to be defined by loose-construction men, outside the letter of the Constitution, and then where would have been strict construction? But Randolph, although he stated that congressional power over the territories was unrestrained, still was not an advocate of making that power a tyranny, and it was he who, in Jefferson's administration, condemned the territorial government of Louisiana and introduced a petition from that region requesting more liberal institutions.

Many a southerner held the protective tariff unconstitutional; but Randolph, the foremost opponent of the tariff, admitted it to be probably within the letter of the law, although he said the true test of constitutionality was not the effect of the act but the intention of the act; a tariff designed primarily to raise revenue, but incidentally protective, although folly, would be within the aim of the Constitution; one designed expressly to exclude foreign products would be contrary to the intention of the founders. To Neale Alexander, he wrote:

The man who supports the Bank and denounces the Tariff as unconstitutional, may take his choice between knave or fool, unless he admits that he is both.

In one case, the power to lay duties, excises, &c., is granted; in the other, no such power is given. The true key is, that the *abuse, under pretence of exercise of any* power (midnight judiciary, &c.,) is unconstitutional. This unlocks every difficulty. Killing a man may be justifiable homicide, chance-medley, manslaughter or murder, according to the motives and circumstances of the case. An unwise, but honest exercise of a power, may be blamed, but it is not unconstitutional. But every usurped power (as the Bank) is so.[10]

There could hardly be better proof than this that Randolph was fully sincere in his strict interpretation of the Constitution. To detail his whole course would be to write a political history; but we may see, at any rate, how able a teacher Randolph was for that later great exponent of the same doctrine, Calhoun.

### 3

Perhaps Randolph's greatest contribution to the cause of a just distribution of governmental powers was his untiring opposition to the centralizing tendencies of the federal government during the period between 1805 and 1820. With the aid only of a few admirers, he waged the fight against internal improvements, the tariff, foreign wars and entanglements, the Bank, and every other measure which threatened the principles of state rights and the planter economy. By the second decade of the century, the South had begun to come round to his stand; during the first years of the 1820's he was more popular than he was at any other period of his life except during the first administration of Jefferson; but, before that, he was braving the storm. In addition to Randolph's native audacity, the sternest of convictions must have been required to withstand popular apathy and congressional hatred. Doubtless Randolph's clear perception that the cause of strict construction and state rights was united with that of the planter economy—that the sundering of the two issues meant death for either—had a sustaining influence.

To state that Randolph and his Old Republicans—sometimes reduced, in the House, to a half-dozen members—carried on the controversy unaided would be an exaggeration, however; they had strange allies, for a time, in the Federalists of New

England. New England, indeed, maintained even more reso-
lutely the doctrines of strict construction and state rights during
the era of the embargo and the war with England. For it appeared to the New Englanders that their region faced ruin in
consequence of the measures of the government at Washington; Randolph, however, perceiving more clearly long-run consequences, declared that the Old Dominion, for all its devotion
to the Virginia dynasty, would pay "so dearly for the war
whistle." He found Quincy, Otis, and Pickering closer to him
then than such Virginians as Thomas Mann Randolph and
John Eppes, to mention no greater names. Among his valuable
correspondence with Josiah Quincy of Massachusetts appears
this revealing letter of January 29, 1814:

> What a game of round-about has been played since I was initiated into
> the mysteries of politics! I recollect the time when to your Mr. Otis, *State
> Rights* were as nothing in comparison with the proud prerogative of the
> Federal government. *Then* Virginia was building an armory to enable
> her to resist *Federal usurpation....* It was always my opinion that Union
> was the means of securing the safety, liberty, and welfare of the con-
> federacy, and not in itself an end to which these should be sacrificed.
> But the question of resistance to any established government is always
> a question of expediency; and the resort ought never to be had to this
> last appeal, except in cases where the grievance does not admit of palliative
> or temporizing remedies. The one is a case to be decided by argument,
> the other by feeling.[11]

To the "good old thirteen States" and their common ties,
Randolph felt a real attachment. He did not gloss over the
perils and disasters of possible disunion. Resistance to injustice,
however justifiable in the abstract, must be only the last resort
of men denied an appeal. Still, this is the ancestor of the fire-
eaters, repeatedly crying out to centralizers and northern industrial interests and western empire-builders that they were pro-
voking no mere human cattle but rather the enormous might
of the planting and slaveholding and free-trading interest.
Sometimes his hints of resistance in the South by armed force
against the injustice of the general government probably should

be considered chiefly a threat calculated to obtain the "temporizing remedies" of which he wrote. He held the states to be sovereign, nevertheless, and free to sever their ties to the Union if tyranny were put upon them. As for Calhoun, armed resistance was for Randolph the last justifiable resort of a community intolerably oppressed.[12] Randolph, in theory, might have been the more ready of these two to evoke force, for he lacked the faith in constitutional guaranties which the Carolinian professed; but when the test of 1832 came, it was Calhoun who dared the issue of war or peace, although Randolph called for Virginian assistance to South Carolina if the Force Act was put into effect. Henry Adams writes of this facet of Randolph's politics in a sentence which displays the acuity which was Adams' so often: "Patrick Henry and Mr. Madison shrank from this last appeal to arms, which John Randolph boldly accepted; and, in his defense, it is but fair to say that a right which has nowhere any ultimate sanction of force is, in law, no right at all."[13]

Yet to the Hartford Convention, Randolph wrote in terms remonstrating though sympathetic, admitting their grievances while entreating them to endure, as Virginia was enduring. He prophesied the ruin secession would bring—an opinion he very probably still held at the time of South Carolinian nullification, nearly two decades later. He remarked, in part:

> When I exhort to further patience—to resort to constitutional means of redress only, I know that there is such a thing as tyranny as well as oppression; and that there is no government, however restricted in its power, that may not, by abuse, under pretext of exercise of its unconstitutional authority, drive its unhappy subjects to desperation. . . . Our Constitution is an affair of compromise between the States, and this is the master-key which unlocks all its difficulties. If any of the parties to the compact are dissatisfied with their share of influence, it is an affair of amicable discussion, in the mode pointed out by the constitution itself, but no cause for dissolving the confederacy.[14]

## The Division of Power

Here is a suggestion of the doctrines of concurrent powers and special constitutional checks which Calhoun was later to develop. But nullification is not implied.

All during these years, the Southside orator declared, his stand was consistent: the defense of the states against federal encroachment, the liberty of the citizen against all encroachment. He would vote for no new tax, for no new accession of power to any division of government.[15] By a curious destiny he found his most formidable adversary in the debates upon these questions of war powers and national expansion to be an intense young South Carolinian, the rising Calhoun, then a War Hawk, filled with nationalistic enthusiasm, a proponent of liberal construction of the Constitution, internal improvements at national expense, defiance of Britain, and the democratic creed of progress. From the beginning of their acquaintance, Randolph treated Calhoun with a respect he very rarely accorded to his enemies—and a suspicion nearly as profound. The high authority of Henry Adams insists that, with the passage of the years, Randolph converted Calhoun. Certainly those concepts of southern unity and peculiar character, of the danger of consolidatory tendencies to the existence of slavery, of the necessary union between strict construction and state rights, of even concurrent powers and an appeal beyond Congress and the Supreme Court—those theories, after 1824 so relentlessly expounded by Calhoun, had been expressed by Randolph ever since he broke with Jefferson. With what seems to have been a touch of the gift for prophecy that was Randolph's, the Virginian singled out this young representative from upcountry South Carolina, in a speech which (for a change) was more an appeal or lecture than a denunciation, as the special object of his plea for the rights of the states. In January, 1816, the dominant party in Congress proposed a revenue program by the terms of which the direct taxation levied during the late war would be retained as a principle and many of the wartime duties continued also. Randolph, the unacknowledged leader of the motley opposition, rose in fury to denounce this proposal, for he detested wars and tariffs with an equal vehemence. Calhoun, in turn, answered Randolph by declaring that federally financed roads and canals were a part of the effort toward an enduring defense of the country, and so was the subsidy to manufactures which the tariff provided. The nation must prepare for war in time of peace. Randolph retorted at his usual length, but in a tone of solemn warning, almost entreaty, which he seldom deigned to employ. Did Randolph, for the moment, spy out his successor in Calhoun? The Roanoke planter's slaves, and many of his constituents, credited wild Jack Randolph—a man who could see devils on the stairs and fancy dead men writing in the next room—with powers more than human. At any rate, in one of those flashes of intuition which startled all his contemporaries, he turned his burning dark eyes upon Calhoun, pointed at him his bony finger, and in his high and piercing voice called upon the young politician to penetrate deeper into the mysteries of politics. Randolph's cadaverous form, his grand gentleman's manner, his strange and wrinkled face, his imagination heightened by the brandy with which he choked the pain from his perpetual sickness—this nervous and sometimes terrible being, with all these attributes of genius and madness intertwined, cried out to the sober back-country Calvinist Calhoun that one must judge of political measures by their distant but immense effect:

I have long believed there was a tendency in the administration of this Government, in the system itself indeed, to consolidation, and the remarks made by the honorable gentleman from South Carolina have not tended to allay any fears I have entertained from that quarter. Make this a simple integral government, said Mr. R., and I subscribe to the doctrines of the honorable gentleman; because they are drawn from the same fountain from which I have drawn my own principles. Mr. R. said he was glad to see that the gentleman had not raked in the kennels (he would say) of democracy, for the principles of which he formed his political creed. But, said Mr. R., ours is not an integral Government, but a Government of States confederated together. He put it to the

Committee, to the gentleman himself, whether the honorable gentleman's principles (which he had demonstrated with an ability honorable to the State he represented, to the House, and to himself) did not go to the destruction of the State governments. It was not, Mr. R. said, from the preference of present good to a little self-denial, that he opposed the system of the gentleman and his political friends. I say, Mr. R. repeated, that these doctrines go to prostrate the State governments at the feet of the General Government. If the warning voice of Patrick Henry had not apprized me long ago, the events of this day would have taught me that this Constitution does not comprise one people, but that there are two distinct characters in them. Mr. R. said, he had been led heretofore to question whether the fact was so; he now believed it as much as any article of his political creed. When speaking of the value of our form of Government, the gentleman might have added to his remarks, Mr. R. said, that whilst in its federative character it was good, as a consolidated Government it would be hateful; that there were features in the Constitution of the United States, beautiful in themselves, when looked at with reference to the federal character of the Constitution, were deformed and monstrous when looked at with reference to consolidation. The gentleman was too deeply read in Aristotle, too well versed in political lore, to deny the fact.[16]

Here, in five minutes' impromptu utterance, was the essence of Calhoun's later creed. "Randolph's answer was one which Calhoun passed over at the time," writes the chief biographer of the Cast-Iron Man, "but to which he paid tribute many years later."[17] The direct tax was adopted, as Randolph, inured to defeat, had quite expected. But Calhoun had begun to listen to him. "John Randolph stands in history as the legitimate and natural precursor of Calhoun," declares Henry Adams with the characteristic bluntness of that family which Randolph called "the American house of Stuart." "Randolph sketched out and partly filled in the outlines of that political scheme over which Calhoun labored so long, and against which Clay strove successfully while he lived,—the identification of slavery with states' rights. All that was ablest and most masterly, all except what was mere metaphysical rubbish, in Calhoun's statesmanship had been suggested by Randolph years before Calhoun began his states' rights career."[18] This speech of Randolph's against the revenue measures of 1816 was the inception of a long and curious relationship between two brilliant and almost fanatic southerners, marked on Calhoun's part by a pondering courtesy, on Randolph's by a suspicion that sometimes descended to flaming public abuse, even while Calhoun, become Vice-President, brooded over the Senate and refused to suppress the invective of Senator Randolph. Two other paragraphs from Randolph's reply to Calhoun are worth examination. In a tenor of that pathos which is a strong characteristic of all his better speeches, Randolph flung at Calhoun a query which in the long run, as the South Carolinian mulled it over, may have converted the Cast-Iron Man to the views of his adversary:

> The question is, whether or not we are willing to become one great consolidated nation, under one form of law; whether the State governments are to be swept away; or whether we have still respect enough for those old respectable institutions to regard their integrity and preservation as part of our policy? I, for one, said Mr. R., cling to them, because I love my country as I do my immediate connexions; for the love of country is nothing more than the love of every man for his wife, child, or friend. I am not for a policy which must end in the destruction, and speedy destruction, too, of the whole of the State governments.

And Randolph proceeded to show how Calhoun's recommendations for preparing for future war—building of roads and encouragement of manufactures by the federal power—would establish precedents ruinous to the sovereignty of the states. "It was his policy, Mr. R. said, to stick to the States in contests arising between them and the General Government—to the people in all collisions between them and the Government, and between the popular branches and the unpopular branches of the Government—he was wrong, however, he said, to call it unpopular; for, unfortunately, its popularity was that which gave it an irresistible weight in this House and in the nation."[19] During the same month, Randolph delivered a speech on the treaty-making power of the President and the Senate, in which he denied that a treaty could override an act of Congress and pointed out the dangers of such a power, were it to be conceded. It destroyed all balancing of authority, within the national government and between the general government and the states, he declared.[20]

But to prolong this survey of Randolph's opinions during those years of lonely struggle, however interesting, is impracticable here. This period of his career ends with the second Missouri debate, in which Randolph took so active a part, denying the right of Congress to refuse to accept the electoral vote of any state in the Union, as he had denied the right of Congress to insist upon the insertion of certain provisions in the constitution of Missouri. By 1821 the South and the adherents of Jefferson, alarmed at the projects of the National Republicans, and convinced, in part, by the warnings of Randolph and his colleagues, had begun to rally to the cause of strict construction and the states. Upon the publication of John Taylor's *Construction Construed and Constitutions Vindicated,* the aged Jefferson, who had been aroused by the Missouri "fire-bell in the night," wrote: "I acknowledge it has corrected some erring opinion into which I had slidden without sufficient examination."[21] William Leigh, referring to some letters he had read, later wrote of Jefferson to Randolph: "The old gentleman seems from this correspondence, to be more alarmed at the rapid and increasing encroachments of the Federal government than I could have imagined."[22] And Jefferson himself wrote to Nathaniel Macon:

You probably have seen in the newspapers a letter of mine recommending Col. Taylor's book to the notice of our fellow-citizens. . . . There are two measures which if not taken, we are undone. 1st, how to check these unconstitutional invasions of states rights by the federal judiciary. How? Not by impeachment in the first instance, but by a strong protestation of both houses of Congress that such and such doctrines, advanced by the supreme court, are contrary to the constitution: and if they afterward relapse into the same heresies, impeach and set the whole adrift. For what was the government divided into three branches, but that each should watch over the others, and oppose their usurpations. 2. to cease borrowing money to pay off the national debt, if this cannot be done without dismissing the army and putting the ships out of commission, have them up high and dry, and reduce the army to the lowest point at which it was ever established.[23]

Randolph—who, like the Adamses, thought most men humbugs—must have experienced a grim pleasure on beholding these symptoms of fright at the tendencies which Randolph had been fighting since 1805. The man of Roanoke enjoyed a degree of triumph and popularity again; no longer was he almost alone in his demand for a nice division of power, and his best speeches upon the subject were made during this period.

On January 31, 1824, Randolph delivered his long speech on the proposed surveys for roads and canals. There has been no better exposition of the argument for strict constitutional construction. First he assailed the passion for attempting to exercise to the utmost every power conceivably granted by the Constitution, and then he launched into a condemnation of the latitudinarians of constitutional interpretation, who took the authority to establish post roads as signifying authority to *build* post roads. By words—"the counters of wise men, the money of fools"—the lovers of political manipulation and governmental spending intend to cajole Americans out of their rights and liberties. The makers of the Constitution had intended to grant Congress only a minimum power over the economy; indeed, if the Constitution when submitted for ratification had included a specific provision for laying a duty of 10 per cent ad valorem on imports, the Constitution never would have been adopted.

Nor had the power to "regulate" commerce ever been intended at the convention as a power to hamper, restrict, or prohibit. "It is rather unfortunate for this argument, that, if it applies to the extent to which the power to regulate foreign commerce has been carried on by Congress, they may prohibit altogether this domestic commerce, as they have heretofore, under the other power, prohibited foreign commerce."[24] Years before, Randolph had pronounced Jefferson's embargo unconstitutional because it constituted a destruction of commerce, no mere regulation. Are these unconstitutional augmentations of power now to be extended over interstate commerce? What might not this usurpation do to the peculiar institution of the Southern States?

Quite as dangerous would be a loose interpretation of the "general welfare" clause, Randolph continued. Commenced by Hamilton, this device was now carried to new extremes by "a new sect" determined to "so far transcend Alexander Hamilton and his disciples, as they out-went Thomas Jefferson, James Madison, and John Taylor of Caroline."[25] Under the pretext of general welfare, anything might be done; there might better be no constitution at all. In a passage glowing with that curious, random wit and learning which Randolph always sandwiched into his most solemn appeals, he proceeded to show that, the principle of "liberal" constitutional construction once conceded, security under law exists nowhere:

But, sir, it is said . . . we have a right to regulate commerce between the several States; and it is argued that "to regulate" commerce is to prescribe the way in which it shall be carried on—which gives, by a *liberal* construction, the power to *construct* the way, that is, the roads and canals on which it is to be carried: Sir, since the days of that unfortunate man, of the German coast, whose name was originally Fyerstein, Anglicized to Firestone, but got, by translation, from that to Flint, from Flint to Pierre-a-Fusil, and from Pierre-a-Fusil to Peter Gun—never was greater violence done to English language, than by the construction, that, under the power to prescribe the way in which commerce shall be carried on, we have the right to construct the way on which it is to be carried. Are gentlemen aware of the colossal power they are giving to the General Government? Sir, I am afraid, that that ingenious gentleman, Mr. McAdam, will have to give up his title to the distinction of the *Colossus of Roads,* and surrender it to some gentlemen of this Committee, if they succeed in their efforts on this occasion. . . .

Nay, we may go further. We may take it into our heads—Have we not the power to provide and maintain a navy? What is more necessary to a navy than seamen? And the great nursery of our seamen is (besides fisheries) the coasting trade—we may take it into our heads, that those monstrous lumbering wagons that now traverse the country between Philadelphia and Pittsburg, stand in the way of the raising of seamen, and may declare that no communication shall be held between these points but coastwise; we may specify some particular article in which alone trade shall be carried on. And, sir, if, contrary to all expectation, the ascendency of Virginia, in the General Government, should again be established, it may be declared that coal shall be carried in no other way than coastwise, &c. Sir, there is no end to the purposes that may be affected under such constructions of power.[26]

Once the principle of "liberal" construction should prevail, in short, the party in power at Washington might manipulate government to its special advantage; continuity of policy in the common interest would give way to the particular and selfish interests of section and class. The Constitution, strictly adhered to, is the shield of minorities; it was therefore of general benefit, for any interest, state, or section, no matter how mighty, is liable some day to find itself a minority. The temptation to use positive law as an instrument of special advantage, once all barriers to its operation should be overthrown, is too great for man to resist; security can be had only if the people agree to restrain the operation of legislatures to provinces clearly defined and if the state and general governments keep themselves rigidly to their prescribed areas of action. Sometimes states had endeavored to encroach on the powers of the federal government, Randolph admitted; this is as dangerous a course as federal encroachment upon the states; the great balance of authority must be preserved. The advocates of omnicompetent legislatures and amorphous constitutions will in the end destroy their own interests as well. But for the present these centralizers are insensate. Having allowed the general government to assume the powers of the purse and the sword, the states discover that everything else they possess is at the mercy of Washington. "We did believe there were some parchment barriers—no! What is worth all the parchment barriers in the world—that there was, in the power of the States, some counterpoise to the power of this body; but, if this bill passes, we can believe so no longer."[27]

A general government restricted to the powers precisely described in the Constitution must necessarily have been a simple and comparatively weak government, unable to plan the national economy or to direct social change in appreciable degree: and this is precisely the sort of government Randolph wanted. Such a government could not have built deliberately a great industrial system in America. Be it so, said Randolph and his associates; they feared and detested the new industrial order. They looked upon society as a spiritual essence which grows healthily only when it grows slowly. If its development is forced, society may become monstrous, spiritually monstrous. Leave economic change, like private life, to the management of Providence and individuals. They abhorred what a recent writer calls "the cult of the colossal."[28] Strict constitutional construction of the commerce power and the general-welfare clause would keep federal authority from molding the national character as the men who run the general government please; in short, the molding of national character would be left to tradition and Providence, which is precisely what Randolph desired. He railed at "planners" of every description. His assertions of the lengths to which construction of the commerce clause may be carried have been entirely sustained by the subsequent course of American history, and the Virginia, the South, and the America he loved have been swept away by the industrial society thus stimulated.

Prescient as Cassandra, Randolph beheld in his imagination this immense standardizing force which glowered from behind "liberal construction"; and, to redress the balance, he summoned up southern sectionalism. Previously contemptuous of many politicians and policies to the south of Virginia, from 1824 onward he relied increasingly upon a self-conscious southern regional interest to furnish a counterpoise for the vast northern industrial interest which had proved too ruthless to be restrained by the Constitution alone. Probably Randolph had been the first statesman to define the South as the quasi-nation bounded by "Mason and Dixon's line" (for which expression he sometimes substituted "south of the Patapsco"); and now he incessantly reminded that region of its distinct and common character:

Should this bill pass, one more measure only requires to be consummated; and then we, who belong to that unfortunate portion of this Confederacy which is south of Mason and Dixon's line . . . have to make up our own minds to perish like so many mice in a receiver of mephitic gas, under the experiments of a set of new political chemists; or we must resort to the measures which we first opposed to British aggressions and usurpations—to maintain that independence which the valor of our fathers acquired, but which is every day sliding from under our feet. I beseech all those gentlemen who come from that portion of the Union to take into serious consideration, whether they are not, by the passage of this bill, precipitately, at least without urgent occasion, now arming the General Government with powers hitherto unknown—under which we shall become, what the miserable proprietors of Jamaica and Barbados are to their English mortgagees, mere stewards—sentinels—managers of slave labor—we ourselves retaining, on a footing with the slave of the West Indies, just enough of the product of our estates to support life, while all the profits go with the course of the Gulf stream. Sir, this is a state of things that cannot last. If it shall continue with accumulated pressure, we must oppose to it associations, and every other means short of actual insurrection. We must begin to construe the Constitution like those who treat it as a bill of indictment, in which they are anxious to pick a flaw—we shall keep on the windward side of treason—but we must combine to resist, and that effectually, these encroachments, or the little upon which we now barely subsist will be taken from us.[29]

"The windward side of treason"—how might this uneasy check upon consolidation and the new economic order be ascertained and persevered in? Randolph referred to two courses of action still open to the states in extremity:

This Government is the breath of the nostrils of the States. Gentlemen may say what they please of the preamble to the Constitution; but this Constitution is not the work of the amalgamated population of the then existing confederacy, but the offspring of the States; and however high we may carry our heads, and strut and fret our hour, "dressed in a little brief authority," it is in the power of the States to extinguish this Government at a blow.[30]

In short, the states might dissolve the general government by refusing to send senators to Washington, so that the lack of a quorum in the upper chamber would make the passing of legislation impossible; or they might refuse to appoint presidential electors and thus obliterate the executive power. Indeed, Randolph is said to have recommended the former course to Clay at the time of the Missouri Compromise.[31] For all the violence of his language on occasion, Randolph was no disunionist, and he would have resorted to these measures only under intolerable provocation; and then, supposing a government to be carried on in defiance of the lack of constitutional authority, forceful resistance would be justified as the final appeal to equity.

Even as he spoke, an opinion on these recourses more extreme than his was beginning to rise in South Carolina. Only three months later, Calhoun's uneasiness at the growing arrogance of industrialism and the North came to a head as a result of the debate over the tariff of 1824. From that time on, Calhoun turned toward strict construction, state rights, southern sectionalism, and conservative measures.[32] South Carolina began to assume that leadership in the struggle against consolidation which Virginia formerly had maintained. The tariff of 1824, frankly protective and brutally indifferent to the southern agricultural interest, was provocation sufficient to rouse to anger men far less irascible than Randolph. Being put in a substantial majority by the congressional reapportionment three years earlier, the congressional party which represented the northern and western protectionists proposed an increase in duties averaging 37 per cent, doubling the previous rate. Agriculture in the Southeastern States, already in great difficulties and reduced to a return of only 2 per cent on investment as compared with the swelling profits of northern industrialism,[33] was awakened to its perilous situation as all the previous exhortations of Randolph and the Old Republicans had never been able to excite that sluggish interest. Once more, after many years of unpopularity as the erratic spokesman of a "lean and proscribed minority," Randolph became the orator of a great and determined part of Congress:

I speak with the knowledge of what I say, when I declare, that this bill is an attempt to reduce the country south of Mason and Dixon's line, and east of the Allegany Mountains, to a state of worse than colonial bondage; a state to which the domination of Great Britain was, in my judgment, far preferable . . . for the British Parliament never would have dared to lay such duties on our imports, or their exports to us, . . . as is now proposed to be laid upon the imports from abroad. . . . It marks us out as the victims of a worse than Egyptian bondage. It is a barter of so much of our rights, of so much of the fruits of our labor, for political power to be transferred to other hands. It ought to be met, and I trust it will be met, in the southern country, as was the Stamp act, and by all those measures, which I will not detain the House by recapitulating, which succeeded the Stamp act, and produced the final breach with the mother country, which it took about ten years to bring about; as I trust in my conscience, it will not take as long to bring about similar results from this measure, should it become a law.[34]

Quoting Burke, Randolph declared all policy suspicious that sacrifices the interest of a part to the alleged good of the whole. This bill was precisely a measure of that description; it was candidly designed for the benefit of special interests at the expense of a minority already hard pressed. The Constitution having been torn up by this majority of protectionists and consolidators who valued immediate gain above the rule of law, the South must be prepared to meet insolent power, if need be, with righteous power. "With all the fantastic and preposterous theories about the rights of man, (the *theories,* not the rights themselves, I speak of,) there is nothing but power that can restrain power. . . . We are proscribed, and put to the ban; and if we do not feel, and feeling do not act, we are bastards to those fathers who achieved the Revolution; then shall we deserve to make our bricks without straw."[35] Forcible resistance to injustice was implicit here; but separation was the remedy only of desperation, and Randolph declared his attachment to the Union—"But there is no magic in this word *union*.... The marriage of Sinbad the sailor, with the corse of his deceased wife, was an union, and just such an union as will this be, if, by a bare majority in both Houses, this bill becomes a law."[36]

He trusted that the President would veto the bill, should it be passed; and if he did not—why, the "Union" is really a confederation which "contains within itself the seeds of preservation, if not of this Union, at least of the individual Commonwealths of which it is composed."[37] Secession was a right undeniable, Randolph maintained, although a desperate remedy.

Self defense is the first law of nature. You drive us into it. You create heats and animosities amongst this great family, who ought to live like brothers; and, after you have got this temper of mind roused among the Southern people, do you expect to come among us to trade, and expect us to buy your wares? Sir, not only shall we not buy them, but we shall take such measures, (I will not enter into the detail of them now,) as shall render it impossible for you to sell them.[38]

He would boycott the "wooden nutmegs" of the North; he would repel northern avarice after the fashion of the Tea Party. This still is resistance "to windward of treason." And then he came to the peroration of this brilliant speech:

We are the eel that is being flayed, while the cook-maid pats us on the head, and cries, with the clown in King Lear, "down, wantons, down!" There is but one portion of the country that can profit by this bill, and from that portion of the country comes this bare majority in favor of it. I bless God that Massachusetts and Old Virginia are once again rallying under the same banner, against oppressive and unconstitutional taxation; for, if all the blood be drawn from out the body, I care not whether it be drawn by the British Parliament or the American Congress—by an Emperor or a King abroad, or by a President at home.[39]

The tariff was passed, of course; and the President did not veto it; and once the new tariff had crushed the valetudinarian maritime interest of Massachusetts, Webster and his state went over to the protectionists, leaving the South solitary in its plea for strict construction and low duties. Four years more Randolph carried on the struggle for state rights and the old Constitution and then relinquished his place in Congress to others; but he was not to be silent during his last years in Southside Virginia.

*4*

Federal appetite for power made a sectionalist of John Randolph. For years he had sneered at the "cotton barons" of the Lower South; he had been enraged by the acquiescence of Georgia and South Carolina in previous measures of consolidation, loose construction, and internal improvements at federal expense; he had disliked the rough and covetous ways of flush times in Alabama and Mississippi; he had liked Massachusetts men of Josiah Quincy's sort far better than the southern War Hawks. But strict construction of the constitution having given way before the innovating and capitalistic majority, he turned now to southern unity as a means of salvation. In 1829 he wrote to Dr. Brockenbrough:

> The operation of this present government, like a debt at usurious interest, must destroy the whole South. It eats like a canker into our very core. South Carolina must become bankrupt and depopulated. She is now shut out of the English market for her rice, with all the premium of dearth in Europe. I am too old to move, or the end of this year should not find me a resident of Virginia, against whose misgovernment I have full as great cause of complaint as against that of the U.S. It has been one mass of *job* and abuse—schools, literary funds, Charlottesville conventions, and their spawn.[40]

Virginia, too, was changing, and even the ardent champion of the Old Dominion's rights could not endure her failings. But it was Virginia, he said in the Virginia Convention later that year, that long had maintained, almost alone, the cause of the states; and to alter the constitution of Virginia would be to endanger the continuance of that opposition to federal usurpation:

# The Division of Power

What provision is there, Mr. Chairman, either in the Constitution of Virginia or the Constitution of the United States, which establishes it as a principle, that the Commonwealth of Virginia should be the sole re-straining and regulating power on the mad and unconstitutional usurpations of the Federal Government? There is no such provision in either;—yet, in practice, and in fact, too, the Commonwealth of Virginia has been, to my certain knowledge, for more than thirty years, the sole counter-poise and check on the usurpations of the Federal Government—so far as they have been checked at all; I wish they had been checked more effectually.

For a long time, our brethren of the South, because we were the fron-tier state of the great Southern division of the Union, were dead to con-siderations to which we have, I fear, awaked too late. Virginia was left alone and unsupported, unless by the feeble aid of her distant offspring, Kentucky. It is because I am unwilling to give up this check, or to diminish its force, that I am unwilling to pull down the edifice of our State Government from the garret to the cellar; aye, to the foundation stone. I will not put in hazard this single good, for all the benefits the warmest advocate of reform can hope to derive from the results of this body.[41]

If to Virginia, as a state, went the credit of this struggle, to Randolph, as a man, the recognition as the prime mover of that course was due; and Randolph was not to abandon the cause in that controversy of which the first mutters were then to be heard; for nullification was in the air.

John Randolph of Roanoke, who rarely forgave a political foe, always distrusted John C. Calhoun, who was to fill, in the years to come, the place that Randolph had occupied in national politics. Perhaps the memory of his debates with Calhoun the War Hawk on the floor of the House made Randolph suspect the permanency of Calhoun's conversion to the ideals for which the man of Roanoke had waged the battle relentlessly; and, like many another southerner, Randolph believed Calhoun to be personally ambitious, ruthlessly ambitious. The South Caro-linian made an effort to obtain Randolph's valuable support, and, for a time, in 1827, almost succeeded. Randolph wrote to Brockenbrough, "I saw the V. P. yesterday. He is in good spirits; he is sustained by a powerful passion."⁴² But later letters show how this slight confidence waned, and Benjamin Perley Poore relates an incident which, accurately told or not, illustrates Randolph's attitude toward the Carolinian. Randolph, who had been accustomed to addressing the Speaker of the House, rose, and exclaimed, "Mr. Speaker! I mean Mr. President of the Senate and would-be President of the United States, which God in his infinite mercy avert."⁴³ But whatever Randolph thought of him, Calhoun must have felt the influence of the Virginian's mind and tongue, both in the House and in the Senate. Henry Adams says that "Randolph converted Calhoun."⁴⁴ Circumstances converted him, too, naturally; but Randolph's statement of the great political issues in America charted the course for Calhoun and his school.

Nullification, however, was not the policy of Randolph; he assailed it as one of those theories of abstract metaphysics he had denounced so often, and, while he upheld vigorously the right of secession, he proclaimed that a state could not remain in the Union and still refuse to obey the Union's laws. He was enraged at Calhoun, moreover, for dividing the South and attacking the leadership of Jackson, upon whom Randolph relied to defend southern interests. After South Carolina's proclamation of nullification, but before Jackson's Force Bill, Randolph wrote to the President: "The infamous conduct of Calhoun and his wretched creatures has damned him and them everlastingly in Virginia, Penna. and New York, and in the West also. Clay has 'trained off.' He has cut his throat with his own tongue."⁴⁵ And a little later he informed Jackson: "I told my noble friend Hamilton in my letter to him (which you shall see) that the throwing over board Mr. Jonah Calhoun was a condition precedent to any aid from *our* quarter, especially from me."⁴⁶ Randolph sent Beverley Tucker to remonstrate, in vain, with Calhoun.⁴⁷

Jackson's proclamation against the nullifiers changed Randolph's sympathies utterly; "nullification was nonsense," but the federal government could not coerce a sovereign state, and Virginia should prepare to come to the aid of threatened South Carolina. Randolph declared himself ready to have his dying body strapped to his horse "Radical" and enter the field against the federal troops;[48] to a friend he spoke of "the ferocious and bloodthirsty proclamation of our Djezzar Pacha," and added:

> The apathy of our people is most alarming. If they do not rouse themselves to a sense of our condition and put down this wretched old man, the whole country is irretrievably ruined. The mercenary troops who have embarked for Charleston have not disappointed me; they are working in their vocation, poor devils! I trust that no quarter will be given to them.[49]

The dying man made a final great effort; he addressed the freeholders at Charlotte Court House, where he had made many a speech for thirty years, and forced down the throats of Jackson men and old Federalists a set of resolutions denouncing the conduct of the President. "Here I remark I am no Nullifier," he said. "The doctrine of nullification is sheer nonsense."[50] But he could not endure Jackson's measures, and the dying orator, with his ruined body and flickering mind, charmed the people of his district into signing the resolutions which declared Virginia to be a sovereign state which had but delegated the exercise of certain powers to federal government; that she retained the right to secede "whenever she shall find the benefits of union exceeded by its evils"; that Jackson had been won over to the cause of every evil influence; that, while the doctrine of nullification was "weak and mischievous," the doctrines of Jackson were equally unfounded and more dangerous; and that the signers approved of the mission of Benjamin Watkins Leigh to South Carolina. The ninth resolution stated that "although we believe that we shall be in a lean and proscribed minority, we are prepared to take up our cross, confident of success under that banner, so long as we keep faith and can have access to the public ear."[51]

Thus John Randolph of Roanoke made his final stand for the rights of the states and against federal encroachment. Even in the passion of these last resolutions, his desire to resort first to consultation and conciliation is conspicuous; for, although secession was a right, it was not a good. For more than a third of a century Randolph had endeavored to maintain what he considered the just distribution of power between federal and state governments; he had given his allegiance to what he thought the only honest construction of the Constitution; and he had attempted, even while rallying the South to resistance against the measures of the nationalists and the North, to remain true to the principles upon which the federal system had been established. Henry Adams writes: "The doctrine of states' rights was in itself a sound and true doctrine; as a starting point of American history and constitutional law, there is no other which will bear a moment's examination."[52] That parchment guaranties could be a permanent barrier against usurpation, Randolph knew to be impossible; but if men could be persuaded that solely by strict fidelity to parchment could tranquillity and union be perpetuated, the ruin he foresaw might be averted. A consolidated government he thought the worst of all evils; and, surely, a consolidated government in this nation—or a government approaching what Randolph would have called consolidation—has proved incompatible with the society he represented. To the cause of local liberties and the guaranties of the federal Constitution he gave all the chivalric valor that was his.

While the nullification quarrel was at its height, the lugubrious man of Roanoke wrote to Harvey: "I could not have believed that the people would so soon have shown themselves unfit for free government. I leave to General Jackson, and the Hartford men, and the ultrafederalists and tories, and the office-holders and office-seekers, their triumph over the liberties of the country. They will stand damned to everlasting fame."[53]

## The Division of Power

The fate of all Randolph's adversaries has not been so bitter as that; and one of them, John Quincy Adams, shares with Randolph the honor of being the most candid and honest public men of their generation. But with respect to political constancy and purity, John Randolph's struggle for a proper division of the powers of government entitles him to a position almost unique among American statesmen.

## CHAPTER FIVE

# The Planter-Statesman

*I*

JOHN TAYLOR of Caroline declared that land is the basis of all wealth and that therefore land deserves power in government.[1] Whether Randolph of Roanoke, the admirer of Smith, Ricardo, and Say, admitted the truth of the first part of this physiocratic contention is doubtful; something more modern is implied in Randolph's political economy; and, indeed, old John Taylor belonged to the generation which preceded Randolph's. But whatever opinion the man of Roanoke held concerning the economic pre-eminence of land, no ambiguity shrouded his conviction that the agricultural life is the best state of society man can ask. Randolph was one of the greatest of the planter-statesmen who filled so large a role in the history of the Southern States, from the time of Washington to the time of Davis; and, among all those memorable names, the agrarian society had no more consistent, shrewd, and fierce defender than John Randolph.

"Defender" is a word chosen deliberately here; for the agricultural interest almost always was reeling before the assault of other interests, and, too often, agriculture lost ground, for all the illustrious muster roll of its partisans. Probably the successive defeats of the farm and the plantation in national political contests were a result neither of any innate weakness of rural people nor yet of timidity on the part of their leaders; the cause lay in the conservative nature of the agricultural interest, which had little to gain from change, while the commercial, financial, and industrial interests were full of youthful vigor and rapacity; agriculture could hardly encroach upon them, but they could extort tribute from agriculture. The agrarian party was generous enough at times, moreover—upon the plea of national security—to sacrifice its own advantage to embargo and tariff, while the other economic interests rarely made such concessions.[2] In the West, it is true, the agricultural interest was so linked with expanding industrial forces, and so heartily in accord with that speculative spirit which has always been a danger to American farming and agricultural life—Tocqueville remarks that an American clears a farm only with the intention of selling it for a profit—that for years the Western States remained the political allies of the industrial and financial North. Before 1824 the rural party was self-conscious and articulate only in the Southeastern States, notably Virginia.

Between 1800 and 1828, between Jefferson and Jackson, the planters and farmers pressingly required a champion in Congress; for although the Virginia dynasty, theoretically fond of the rural ideal, and the Republican party, professedly representative of the agricultural interest, maintained control of national politics during the greater portion of this era, still the agricultural economy was exposed to a series of distressing blows all during these years. The farmer always tends to be weaker politically than his numbers seem to indicate. "It is the choicest bounty to the ox," said Randolph, "that he cannot play the fox or the tiger; so it is to one of the body of agriculturalists that he cannot skip into a coffee-house and shave a note with one hand, while with the other he signs a petition to Congress portraying the wrongs and grievances and sufferings he endures, and begging them to relieve him."[3] Lacking the collective cunning and proximity to administration which commercial and industrial forces possessed, the country population was badly prepared to make a stand in Congress. Who was to be their spokesman at Washington? Old John Taylor, that indefatigable writer of treatises, entered Congress with reluctance and departed with alacrity, for he was no popular orator; Jefferson and his successors, however much they praised the life of the farmer, found themselves compelled to pursue policies which left that farmer in a state nearly as disastrous as that in which Jefferson was to find his own lands; Nathaniel Macon and other planter-legislators, great and small, had the requisite devotion but not the requisite genius. The duty fell to John Randolph.

Acerbity of temper and indifference to popularity were flaws which kept Randolph from being a really successful leader of the opposition; but in some other ways he was admirably qualified to maintain the responsibility. He could command public attention—like a necromancer fascinating a snake—in a way no other man of his time could. He could join to the agricultural party other factions which, for a time, had the same objectives: the slavery interest, the state-rights thinkers, and on occasion even the commercial classes of New England. He was himself a successful planter, supervising the cultivation of his thousands of acres; he lived like a pre-Revolutionary Virginia gentleman, bumping over the wretched roads in his old-fashioned English coach, and his slaves rode blooded horses; but he inhabited a two-room cabin and spent the greater part of each year in the oppressive routines of growing tobacco and grains. More, he was devoted by inheritance and principle to the society of the country gentleman and the Virginia landlord. The agricultural ideal occupied as important a place in his system as in Jefferson's, though Randolph's ideal was the old Tidewater life and Jefferson's a yeoman population destined never really to develop as the President hoped.

In some ways a very practical man, Randolph was a severe critic of the rural life he defended, just as he criticized all that he loved. To Josiah Quincy he wrote of "the sordid cares of a planter," to which he was condemned every long and dreary winter: "They remind me of Cromwell, when he turned farmer at St. Ives; for without vanity I may compare myself to what Oliver was *then,* and may with truth declare, that my 'mind, superior to the low occupations to which I am condemned, preys upon itself.' "[4] Randolph's solitary and half-mysterious existence as a Roanoke planter must have had its effect upon his delicate temperament; even while he was still living at Bizarre, away from the shadows of Roanoke, his half-brother, Henry St. George Tucker, wrote to James M. Garnett of Randolph's brooding bitterness: "It is manifest that his solitude has great influence upon his feelings."[5] Yet probably Randolph could have endured no other life; certainly his detestation of towns, his revolt against social mediocrity, and his devotion to field sports would have made Tucker's life as a successful Winchester lawyer anathema to him. In the view of Randolph, Macon, Stanford, and William Leigh, of southern Virginia and northern North Carolina, only in the country, on his own land and free from debt, did a man experience real liberty; and only such men, as a class, were competent to determine the policies of the state.

What did Randolph believe to be the ideal agricultural economy? We have remarked that he found his model in the image of pre-Revolutionary Virginia; Jefferson sought for his in the visions of an equalitarian future. Jefferson's successful campaign for the abolition of entail and primogeniture was intended to equalize landholding, to establish upon a broad base a state—perhaps a nation—of freeholders, small farmers, each nearly self-sufficient economically, producing their foodstuffs and the bulk of their other necessities. Labor on these holdings was to be chiefly that of freemen, the possessors. Such an economy never did come to prevail in Virginia; and, while the radical revision of the laws of descent did indeed greatly diminish the prosperity and influence of the old families that had led the Old Dominion, still it failed signally to produce a general equalization of landowning. Tocqueville attributes to the American abolition of entail and primogeniture a very great share in the restlessness, cupidity, and wistful materialism of the American people; it destroyed one of those artifices which, in Burke's phrase, enable "generation to link with generation" and distinguish men from "the flies of a summer."

Randolph, on the other hand, roundly damned this alteration of the laws of descent; that act of innovation had enervated the great families which contributed, in previous generations, so much to Virginia's glory. Frequently he referred to this topic and once wrote, while in Europe, to Brockenbrough, that he had no hope for a restoration of the ancient Virginian spirit, "the state of society and manners which existed in Virginia half a century ago; I should as soon expect to see the Nelsons, and Pages, and Byrds, and Fairfaxes, living in their palaces, and driving their coaches and sixes; or the good old Virginia gentlemen in the assembly, drinking their twenty and forty bowls of rack punches, and madeira, and claret, in lieu of a knot of deputy sheriffs and hack attorneys, each with his cruet of whiskey before him, and puddle of tobacco-spittle between his legs."[6] Yet he fought for the old ways toward which he was already looking back with a nostalgia so many Virginians later were to share.

The old Virginian life Randolph praised had not been simply a society dominated by great slaveholding landlords. He spoke contemptuously of Wade Hampton and his fellows as "cotton barons" and declared the real substance of society to be the independent planters and farmers of small freeholds, which class he eulogized in the Virginia Convention of 1829, speaking of "the good old Virginia planter—the man who lived by hard work, and who paid his debts."[7] That which Randolph desired was a society with a great number of small freeholders to furnish the bulk of the governing class and a scattering of wealthier and better-educated great planters to furnish suitable leadership for the commonwealth. Indeed, his own congressional district was made up of such a society, with a few great landholders like Randolph, the Carringtons, and the Leighs, and a numerous class of less wealthy landowners who, like the Bouldins, sometimes achieved important political office. Randolph, like Jefferson, believed in an aristocracy of nature, not of station; but he thought that aristocracy of nature largely determined by the gifts of good family and of possession of property. Jefferson apparently held that his agricultural class should devote its energies principally to the raising of foodstuffs for their own consumption rather than to a money crop like tobacco. While Randolph raised the greater part of the food for his slaves on his own lands, still tobacco was his chief crop, and he was the foremost advocate of the old trade with England, exchanging Virginian agricultural staples for British manufactures.[8] Although Jefferson wrote his famous phrase comparing cities to the sores of the body and recommended an economy strictly agricultural, trading with the "workshops of Europe," this stand of his was altered after the embargo days, and he came to recommend the encouragement of American factories. This, Randolph could not tolerate; he would not buy from the North, out of resentment at protective tariffs, and he even sent his books to England to be bound. As in Jefferson's literary taste, a certain old-fashioned element lingered in Jefferson's economic thought: the President spoke of the advantage in international trade as lying in the disposal of "national surpluses," in his letters to Du Pont de Nemours and others.[9] Randolph, much read in Smith and Ricardo, perceived more distinctly the nature of specialization and the economic advantages of unrestricted international commerce and contended that America was as unsuited for really profitable manufacturing as England was for really profitable agriculture.[10]

Such, then, was Randolph's specific for a satisfactory agricultural society—concepts shared by the Old Republicans. Randolph failed to gain the restoration or perpetuation of his system; but so did Jefferson fail to achieve his agrarian ideal. The Old Republicans failed because they were in an irremediable political minority; because they could not rid themselves of the burden of Negro slavery; and because, very possibly, Malthus' geometrical increase of population was against them—overpopulation, the problem of problems. Their system of landholding was suited to a static population but hardly to a swelling one; and even the rapid advance of the agricultural frontier could not preserve their nation from the necessity of adopting a complicated economy of large-scale manufactures, intricate finance, rapid transportation, and urban life. The Republicans might have retorted that the swelling of population, through immigration and commerce, was deliberately encouraged by the classes and regions which stood to gain by change; but it was too much to expect mankind not to fill a void as rapidly as air fills a vacuum. Desperately the successors of the Old Republicans endeavored to maintain their position by the acquisition of western territories to be amalgamated with the southern agricultural system; and the very endeavor brought closer the war which was to strike down their society. Time and space were against the planter-statesmen. But in many ways the life they sought to perpetuate was good; not a few men would think it a better state of society than that our age must accept; and they are hardly to be censured for standing like men for the old ways. For Cato to stand against Caesar and the forces that Caesar represented was hopeless; but it was not ridiculous. No fatal weakness existed in the Old Republicans' economy per se; but for them the time was out of joint. Their principles of public and private conduct are not invalidated by time's annihilaton of the economic system in which their ideas developed. On the management of government, the conduct of foreign relations, and the commercial policy of the state, Randolph and his fellows spoke out boldly to defend the plantation. Although the plantation is gone, there remains a need for honest politics, intelligent statecraft, and sound public economics. In Randolph's career is exhibited the doomed course of the plantation-politicians, and in his principles are elements still worth attention in this very different epoch.

# The Planter-Statesman

*2*

Their most consistent spokesman, Randolph, permanently defined the platform of the planter-statesmen when he told the House of Representatives, early in 1813:

Is it necessary for me at this time of day to make a declaration of the principles of the Republican party? Is it possible that such a declaration could be deemed orthodox when proceeding from lips so unholy as those of an excommunicant from that church? It is not necessary. These principles are on record; they are engraved upon it indelibly by the press and will live as long as the art of printing is suffered to exist. It is not for any man at this day to undertake to change them; it is not for any men, who then professed them, by any guise or circumlocution to conceal apostacy from them, for they are there—there in the book. . . . What are they? Love of peace, hatred of offensive war, jealousy of the State Governments toward the General Government; a dread of standing armies; a loathing of public debt, taxes, and excises; tenderness for the liberty of the citizen; jealousy, Argus-eyed jealousy, of the patronage of the President.[11]

From the advocacy of these principles, Randolph and his faction did not retreat. They had been the principles of Jefferson and his devotees in 1800, Randolph declared; they remained the principles of true Republicans. A simple, economical, limited, peaceful government was the only government consistent with the society they represented—a government fit for a stable, rural nation. But there remains a great deal of room for increase of these virtues in the state in our own more complex society.

Always prominent in the Old Republican creed was a demand for purity and simplicity in public affairs, retrenchment and reform. The sincerity of Randolph's long campaign against profligacy, corruption, and time-serving in governmental affairs never has been successfully impeached, even by his most hostile critics. From his great Yazoo speeches to his duel with Clay, Randolph was the dread of every self-seeker in Congress; and although some writers have believed Randolph's ideals of purity impossible of attainment and his stand as a

( 89 )

political St. Michael too top-lofty, none has condemned his general course of action. Randolph and the other Old Republicans were men of private honesty, of economical and self-sufficient habits; they saw no reason why private morals should not be public morals or why the government should plunder, or be plundered, when the citizen should not. Out of their very nature they were opposed to regular party organization, to all the intricacies of party machinery, to caucus and convention. Their dislike for practical politics, then, was another obstacle between them and success.

Although they were resolute supporters of the rights of private property, they did not hold that private property dishonestly obtained had a clear title against government; as John Taylor wrote, "If Jugurtha had been rich enough to buy Rome, ought the nation to have submitted to the sale, because the bargain was made with the government?"[12] Thus it was that Randolph denounced the Yazoo land companies and prevented, while he was in Congress, the compensation of those associations. That Jefferson did not take a firm stand against the Yazoo speculators helped provoke John Randolph's initial opposition to his administration, and the Roanoke orator detested Madison in the belief that he was a "Yazoo man." Perhaps the most shocking episode in the history of Congress, Yazoo left a rift between Jefferson and his congressional leader which never could be bridged. Speculative land companies had obtained immense grants of territory from a Georgia legislature they had corrupted by shameless bribery; a subsequent legislature indignantly repealed the land grants; and those companies of speculators in lands along the Yazoo River appealed to Congress to compensate them for their losses. The same measures toward persuasion which had been exercised in Georgia now appeared in Washington, the notorious Gideon Granger, postmaster-general, presuming to lobby for the bill on the floor of the House—until Randolph denounced him as one accustomed to "buy and sell corruption in the gross." Jefferson and the northern Republicans winked at the affair, out of expediency (indeed, in later years Jefferson actually would have liked to appoint Granger to the Supreme Court); but Randolph and the Old Republicans now began to take shape as a faction, outraged at this violation of the purity of the Republican party. They never would compromise with great selfish interests; they had a terror of what has since come to be known as the "pressure group."

This was barefaced corruption; but the Old Republicans dreaded scarcely less that double-dealing, secrecy, and pretense in public affairs which come with governmental meddling in economic concerns. "I was not born into this order of things, and I will never consent, voluntarily, to become the vassal of a privileged order of military and monied men, by whom, as by a swarm of locusts, the produce of my land is to be devoured, and its possessor consigned to indigence and scorn. He who will not assert his place in society deserves to be trampled under foot."[13]

Faithful to Randolph's declaration, the Old Republicans asserted their place with great wrath and did their best to prevent the devouring of the produce of their lands; even when the government was in their own hands, they did not trust it. In 1803, when he exerted vast influence upon the course of the federal administration, Randolph wrote to Nicholson: "To me the tendency of the power of appointment to office (no matter to what individual it may be trusted) to debauch the nation and to create a low, dirty, time-serving spirit is a ... serious evil."[14]

Going beyond their assault on the abuse of public funds, the Old Republicans demanded strict economy in lawful and necessary expenditures. Randolph's opposition to the proposal of a sword for the adventurer Eaton and to a mausoleum for Washington, while in these days they may seem petty wrangling, were matters of principle; for Randolph believed that if governmental appropriations for baubles were not checked at the outset, they never would be halted. One of his chief objections to the program of internal improvements was that it would require funds which should be used instead to pay the federal debt, which he considered a drain upon the public for the benefit of special interests: "Let us leave the profits of labor in the pockets of the people, to rid them of that private embarrassment under which they so extensively suffer, and apply every shilling of the revenue, not indispensable to the exigencies of the Government, to the faithful discharge of the public debt, before we engage in any new schemes of lavish expenditure."[15] From an early period, the Old Republicans foresaw that progressive inflation of credit and currency which has been a prominent characteristic of the American economy since the foundation of the Republic. Financial inflation means instability and the ruin of old ways; the innate conservatism of the Old Republicans, professed levelers though they were, revolted at the prospect of a society forever in flux and change.

Debt, Randolph maintained, was slavery; and once he startled the House by crying out, "Mr. Speaker, I have discovered the philosopher's stone. It is this, sir—Pay as you go! Pay as you go!"[16] In 1828, Macon, who was lodging with Randolph in Washington, wrote to a friend an expression of his and Randolph's view of the course of Congress:

Almost every bill reported is to take money out of the Treasury or taxes from the U.S. It must be thought by some, I wish not by too many, that a public debt is a public blessing & all who live on the public, no doubt think, the more taxes the better, & that every tax adds to industry, & the harder people are put to it, the more easy they will be to govern; from such I wish to be delivered & hope the country may be free from them.[17]

Something of a mid-twentieth-century flavor is in this paragraph. Randolph might have expressed such an opinion more elegantly than did his old friend from North Carolina, but he would have put it no less energetically.

But he was not so fanatically devoted to economy that he

neglected stability in government; for when it was suggested at the Virginia Convention that the number of state representatives be reduced in order to cut legislative expenses, he opposed this false saving: "These savings made by paring down the Legislature, and lopping off the Council, may not prove to be true economy. Remember the fable—if the sheep will not spare enough of their fleece to feed the dogs, they may have to spare the whole of it, and the carcass to boot, to the wolf."[18]

And at this same constitutional convention of 1829, Randolph aptly expressed his whole distrust of government, with its passion for positive law, innovation, and regulation, with its powers of corruption and exploitation, with its demand for haste and uniformity:

I am much opposed, said Mr. R., except in a great emergency—and then the Legislative machine is always sure to work with sufficient rapidity —the steam is then up—I am much opposed to this "dispatch of business." The principles of free government in this country, (and if they fail—if they should be cast away—here—they are lost forever, I fear, to the world,) have more to fear from armies of legislators, and armies of Judges, than from any other, or from all other causes. Besides the great manufactory at Washington, we have twenty-four laboratories more at work, all making laws. In Virginia we have now two in operation, one engaged in making ordinary legislation, and another *hammering* at the fundamental law. Among all these lawyers, Judges, and Legislators, there is a great oppression on the people, who are neither lawyers, Judges, nor Legislators, nor ever expect to be—an oppression barely more tolerable than any which is felt under the European Governments. Sir, I never can forget, that in the great and good book to which I look for all truth and all wisdom, the book of Kings succeeds the book of Judges.[19]

This attitude it is which, in large degree, clears the Old Republicans from any imputation of seeking advantage for themselves or their class in their stand against power in the state. They fought for the planter life, for the life they thought best; but they did not ask special advantage for that agricultural society, unlike the farm bloc of a later day. They asked only to be left unmolested, allowed to buy and sell in a free market, not to be taxed for the benefit of other interests, not to be forced into another mode of life. All government, said Randolph, was menacing; the only safety for every interest and class and section lay in limitation of the power of governments, in jealous supervision of governmental operation. Let government leave men to their own concerns and be economical, equitable, and honest. Randolph's principles of political purity and social organization gave way to a different order of things chiefly because other great interests, reckless of such concepts, found it advantageous to conduct government along very different lines; and although the Old Republicans experienced temporary victories in their struggle for honesty and simplicity, their campaign was a stubborn retreat. From 1805 onward, Randolph's school of the agricultural interest and the earlier Republican idealism was hopelessly outnumbered.

*3*

In order to flourish, or even to exist, the society of the planters was dependent upon the guaranties of a strictly constructed Constitution, upon a reasonably free trade with the world, upon simple and austere government, and upon lasting peace. From all these motives, and also because men of the sturdy conservative convictions held by the Old Republicans were naturally lovers of tranquillity and foes of aggression, Randolph's faction stood opposed to war and foreign alliances. They resisted as best they could the approach of the War of 1812; and, when apparently the struggle had become inevitable, John Randolph, Stanford, and a few other congressmen struggled almost unaided against the tide. Randolph experienced his sole defeat for a seat in the House in consequence of his opposition; but events seemed to vindicate his conduct, and he was returned by his constituents, in the following election, to continue for the remainder of his career the advocacy of political isolation and economic internationalism for America.

From his Jacobin days in 1797, when Randolph opposed war

with France, until the days of the Panama Congress in 1826, Randolph was the foe of all proposals for hostilities or foreign entanglements—if one excepts some remarks of his recommending retaliation against England, after the "Chesapeake" affair. From the inception of the embargo until the last echoes of the second war with England had died, the danger of war, together with denunciations of the American restrictive commercial policy, was the great theme of his speeches. His remarks—some of them nearly as pertinent now as then—are worth sampling with a view toward their relation to his planter society.

In John Adams' administration Randolph called the federal troops "ragamuffins," and in Jackson's administration he sneered at them as "mercenaries." He declared them a threat to the rights of the states, for he placed his reliance for state sovereignty chiefly in the physical superiority of the states to the federal government and not in parchment guaranties; moreover, they were a drain upon the public purse. His own plan for efficiently arming the militia, and substituting flying trains of artillery for permanent harbor fortifications and Jefferson's gunboats, never was adopted; but it had merit, John Taylor writing of it: "Mr. Randolph's proposal ... is the most effectual, principled, and grand measure, which has been introduced since the government has been in operation. He ought to nurse his popularity in Congress, if for no other end, but to carry the one point."[20]

Nursing popularity was a talent in which Randolph was totally deficient; instead, sarcasm and terror were his weapons. He opposed the increase of the national army with great bitterness; his speeches from 1807 until the close of hostilities with Britain expound his views with a thoroughness that cannot be imitated here.[21] On November 21, 1812, he delivered one of his most significant speeches on the question of military establishments and preparations for war, holding that he derived his principles from the old and true doctrines of the Republican party and that he would not yield them for the sake of popularity.²² He declared that Britain was our shield against Napoleonic tyranny; he exposed the "agrarian cupidity" of the West, which sought war in order to provide markets for its hemp and foodstuffs; and he proclaimed that the Republicans were following the path disastrously trodden by the Federalists:

There is a fatality, sir, attending plentitude of power. Soon or late, some mania seizes upon its possessors; they fall from the dizzy height, through the giddiness of their own heads. Like a vast estate, heaped up by the labor and industry of one man, which seldom survives the third generation, power gained by patient assiduity, by a faithful and regular discharge of its attendant duties, soon gets above its own origin. Intoxicated by their own greatness, the federal party fell. Will not the same causes produce the same effects now as then? Sir, you may raise this army, you may build up this vast structure of patronage, this mighty apparatus of favoritism; but—"lay not the flattering unction to your souls"—you will never live to enjoy the succession. You sign your political death warrant. . . .

He was not surprised at the war-spirit which is manifesting itself in gentlemen from the South. In the year 1805–06, in a struggle for the carrying-trade of belligerent colonial produce, this country was most unwisely brought into collision with the great powers of Europe. By a series of most impolitic and ruinous measures, utterly incomprehensible to every rational sober-minded man, the Southern planters, by their own votes, succeeded in knocking down the price of cotton to seven cents, and of tobacco (a few crops excepted) to nothing, and in raising the price of blankets (of which a few would not be amiss in a Canadian campaign), coarse woollens, and every article of first necessity, three or four hundred per cent. And, now that by our own acts we have brought ourselves into this unprecedented condition, we must get out of it in any way but by an acknowledgement of our own want of wisdom and forecast. But is that the true remedy? Who will profit by it? Speculators; a few lucky merchants who draw prizes in the lottery; commissaries and contractors. Who must suffer by it? The people. It is their blood, their taxes, that must flow to support it. . . .²³

In speech after speech, Randolph demonstrated how ruinous the war was for his own Virginia—more ruinous even than the nonimportation and embargo acts. And the young men of Virginia, he added, their prospects of employment and independence ruined, drift away to Washington, there "dancing attendance for a commission." War and an omnipotent administration breed similar servility in politicians of all parties, who begin to sink into "very good courtiers"; thus effective opposition withers, and free government with it.[24]

There is evident here Randolph's dread of the corrupting power of government in general and the federal government in particular. The greatest danger did not come from abroad, maintained Randolph; it was domestic and a real threat to liberty. As he replied to Calhoun in 1816:

> The gentleman had represented this country as contending with Great Britain for existence. Could the honorable gentleman, or any other man, Mr. R. asked, believe that we would ever have a contest with any nation for existence? No, said Mr. R., we hold our existence by charter from the great God who made this world; we hold it in contempt of Great Britain— I speak of civil freedom—I am addressing myself to one who understands these distinctions. We do not hold our right to physical being or political freedom by any tenure from Europe; yet we hold our tenure of civil liberty by a precarious tie, which must be broken; for, from the disposition to follow the phantom of honor, or from another cause, this country is fairly embarked on a course of policy like that which is pursued by other governments in Europe.[25]

Randolph's unyielding opposition to war and expansion and his advocacy of the most unpopular of courses at that time brought general condemnation upon him; the town of Randolph, in Georgia, named in his honor, was renamed Jasper, in wrath;[26] and even the poets assailed him. Referring to his habit of sucking stick candy in the House chamber, one wrote of Randolph:

> When *bitter* Randolph *candy* ate,
> We wondered, one and all!
> But, see the strange decree of fate
> Turn *Candy* into *Gall!*[27]

Randolph endured the storm, and the disasters of the war with England proved him a true prophet and restored him to a measure of favor; thereafter he pursued relentlessly his attacks on intervention in foreign quarrels. Such intervention would disrupt the finances of the country, he knew; it would divert attention from disturbed and pressing domestic affairs; it would endanger, by the possible exercise of the treaty power, the guaranties of the Constitution and the authority of the House. In the debate on the Greek question and in that on the Panama Congress, he delivered particularly important speeches, and, since it is not possible to review his whole course in defense of American political isolation, we may obtain a fair picture of his stand by glancing at a part of one of his speeches on the former subject. The passion for intervening in the concerns of Europe and Latin America led, he maintained, to unconstitutional projects and policies, to ends and means never contemplated by the framers of the Constitution; he, who before 1812 had declared, "We will come out of this war without a Constitution," believed this would be the result of foreign meddling short of war, as well.

It has once been said, of the dominions of the King of Spain—thank God! it can no longer be said—that the sun never set upon them. Sir, the sun never sets on ambition like this; they who have once felt its scorpion sting are never satisfied with a limit less than the circle of our planet. I have heard, sir, the late corruscation in the Heavens attempted to be accounted for by the return of the Lunar cycle, the moon having got back into the same relative position in which she was nineteen years ago. However this may be, I am afraid, sir, that she exerts too potent an influence over our legislation. . . .

Let us, said Mr. R., adhere to the policy laid down by the second, as well as the first founder of our Republic—by the Camillus, as well as Romulus, of the infant state—to the policy of peace, commerce, and honest friendship with all nations, entangling alliances with none; for to entangling alliances you must go, if you once embark in such projects as this. And with all his British predilections, Mr. R. said, he suspected he should, whenever that question should present itself, resist as strongly an alliance with Great Britain as with any other power. We are sent here, said he, to attend to the preservation of the peace of this country, and not to be ready, on all occasions, to go to war whenever anything like what in common parlance is termed *a turn up* takes place in Europe.

I can, however, assure the Committee, for one, that the public burdens on those whom I represent here (though they are certainly better off than those to the North and the West of them: that is till you come to the favored states, where the interest of the public debt is paid and where almost all the public moneys are disbursed)—their burdens, sir, are as great as they can bear, because their private engagements are greater than they can discharge—and if this is not a self-evident proposition, I am at a loss to know what can be such. And this universal distress in the country has been the effect of freaks of legislation in the past. I do not deny but there may be some who have drawn great prizes in the lottery, but that is not the case with the great mass of the nation. And what *is this* scheme but a lottery? If it should end in war, there will be more great prizes to be drawn, but it will be for me, for those whom I represent, to pay them. . . .

For my part, I would sooner put the shirt of Nessus on my back than sanction these doctrines—such as I never heard from my boyhood until now. They go the whole length. If they prevail, there are no longer any Pyrenees—every bulwark and barrier of the Constitution is broken down; it is become a *tabula rasa,* a *carte blanche,* for every one to scribble on it what he pleases.[28]

Randolph always could sum up his own views more concisely and more eloquently than another could hope to do; and this speech expressed the dislike of the Old Republicans for governmental measures which went beyond the boundaries of the United States, containing within the space of a few thousand words probably the most able refutation of imperialism that has been heard in Congress. War and imperialism meant the undermining of the society and the Constitution for which Randolph and his friends stood; they meant the economic ruin of their institutions; and they meant that spirit of managing other men's affairs which was so repugnant to these lovers of freedom. It was the War of 1812 which struck an awful blow at their cause, and it was a later war which crushed them to earth.

### 4

In 1808 John Brockenbrough wrote to Randolph: "Patriotism is a mighty precious thing when it costs nothing, but the mass of mankind consider it a very foolish thing when it curtails their self-indulgence."[29] This was during the days of Jefferson's embargo. The Old Republicans, in whom there was little of self-indulgence and a great deal of true patriotism, opposed with all their strength what they considered the ruinous stifling of their economy; and not long after Brockenbrough wrote, the mass of the people, long faithful to the Jeffersonian program, began to turn toward repeal of the prohibition of commerce. For once the Old Republican school triumphed, and they were to win other victories of this sort—in the South, at least. Essential in the Old Republican program was opposition to all regulation of commerce and finance by the federal government—opposition to the embargo and its kindred measures, to the tariff, to the Bank of the United States. Gradually the Old Republicans and their political inheritors brought the majority of the electorate in the Southern States to adopt this hostility toward federal control of trade and industry.

The fear and hatred of restrictive measures and special legislative privilege to economic interests, which had been perhaps the chief characteristic of the Republican party in the first Congress, were kept alive from the second administration of Jefferson to the first administration of Jackson principally by the Old Republicans. The Virginia dynasty and the National Republicans came to look with a most favorable eye upon the protective tariff, the neomercantile system, and even the federally chartered Bank. The Old Republicans saw the doom of their institutions in such establishments, for they knew that wealth, and power with it, would flow to other classes and other regions than their own were those policies to continue; and they thought such a society far inferior to theirs. Not only would there be these economic consequences, but the constitutional precedents set by such a loose interpretation of federal authority would demolish utterly strict construction; and strict construction was an end in itself with these lovers of liberty. John Taylor expressed their viewpoint at great length and with admirable strength in his books; but it is worth our time to see what Randolph's more eloquent tongue had to say.

John Randolph's great speech, in 1806, against Gregg's Resolution, commenced his onslaught upon those restrictions on exports and taxes on imports which would ruin his Old Virginia. Randolph's economics were the doctrines of the classical school, and their consistency was unassailable. Calhoun opposed them, in his earlier years, because he considered domestic manufacturing necessary for national strength in war; but he did not deny that Randolph's premises were economically sound, laying aside questions of political expediency. No one could successfully deny the fact; and certainly no one could successfully meet Randolph in a debate on the question. The argument on Gregg's Resolution, however, was not so much a question of economic principle as it was of the constitutionality of restraint of trade and of its possible effect upon the matter of war or peace. Said Randolph:

As in 1798 I was opposed to this species of warfare, because I believed it would raze the constitution to its very foundation—so, in 1806, I am opposed to it, and on the same grounds. No sooner do you put the constitution to this use—to a test which it is by no means calculated to endure—than its incompetency becomes manifest, and apparent to all. I fear, if you go into a foreign war for a circuitous, unfair carrying-trade, you will come out without your Constitution. Have you not contractors enough yet in this House? Or do you want to be overrun and devoured by commissaries and all the vermin of contract? I fear, sir, that what are called the "energy men" will rise up again; men who will burn the parchment. We shall be told that our Government is too free; or, as they would say, weak and inefficient. Much virtue, Sir, in terms! That we must give the President power to call forth the resources of the nations. That is to filch the last shilling from our pockets—to drain the last drop of blood from our veins.[30]

Yet Gregg's Resolution to forbid importation from Great

Britain and her possessions was as nothing in comparison with Jefferson's embargo, soon to follow. Randolph supported the embargo when it first was introduced in the House, but, after realizing its purpose, voted against it; he had thought it designed only as a temporary measure, which he previously had recommended, for securing American shipping in American harbors before undertaking retaliation against Britain or France. But an indefinite suspension of commerce was wholly another matter; Randolph thought the first form of embargo to be a simple regulation of commerce and therefore constitutional; the second, however, amounted to a prohibition or destruction of commerce and did not accord with the spirit of the commerce clause in the Constitution. For its duration, Randolph assailed the embargo; in its comparatively short span of existence, it did incalculable harm to the agrarian cause, since it ruined half of Virginia and stimulated the manufacturers of New England and the Middle Atlantic States, which demanded tariff protection once the embargo vanished.

Randolph's assaults on the embargo and that greater evil, the war, which followed it, are matters of political history; both events hastened the decline of his Virginia and led to the establishment of that national mercantile policy he so deplored— the protective tariff. He proclaimed that "the embargo, like Achilles' wrath, was the source of our Illiad of woes!"[31] To Brockenbrough he wrote of "the exploded mercantile system, revived and fastened, like the Old Man of the Sea, around our necks." In 1816 he delivered one of the most searching criticisms of that policy, during the discussion of the tariff bill. It was nothing more than a system of bounties to manufacturers, he said with passion, "to encourage them to do that which, if it be advantageous to do at all, they will do, of course, for their own sakes." The productive labor of the country would be distorted and molded into a thousand fantastic shapes to suit the intent and the profit of these special interests. It was simply a question of whether a planter would consent to be taxed to enable another man to set up a spinning jenny. Randolph would sell in the best market and buy in the cheapest and never would agree to this intricate neomercantilism of bounties, even though the proponents of protection should agree to establish bounties for the raising of tobacco, too. The agriculturalist bore the brunt of the war and taxation. The agriculturalist, that great stable element in society, was to be pillaged for the benefit of a class of speculators and note-shavers:

> The agriculturalist has his property, his lands, his all, his household goods to defend; and like that meek drudge, the ox, who does the labor and plows the ground, and then, for his reward, takes the refuse of the farmyard, the blighted blades and the mouldy straw, and the mildewed shocks of corn for his support;—while the commercial speculators live in opulence, whirling in coaches and indulging in palaces; to use the words of Dr. Johnson, coaches which fly like meteors and palaces which rise like exhalations. Even without your aid, the agriculturalists are no match for them. Alert, vigilant, enterprising and active, the manufacturing interest are collected in masses and ready to associate at a moment's warning for any purpose of general interest to their body. . . . The cultivators, the patient drudges of other orders of society, are now waiting for your resolution; for on you it depends whether they shall be left further unhurt or be, like those in Europe, reduced, *gradatim,* and subjected to another squeeze from the hard grasp of power.[32]

Despite all its passion, this defense of the agrarian society was as unavailing as most such pleas since Randolph's time. His remarks upon the tariff of 1824, already quoted partially in a previous chapter, were similar in vein: England, he said, possessed a natural advantage in manufacturing; she was welcome to it, for that condition of society meant only misery for the bulk of her inhabitants.[33] He fought the tariff throughout the last year of his congressional career, at the time his colleague Macon wrote to Edwards: "I have heard that the tariff would be taken up today or tomorrow in the H. of R. We must war old cloathes, & put patch on patch, & not be ashamed, provided we owe nothing, though we may not be dressed in the fashion, there is no better fashion, than to be out of debt."[34] Such was the simplicity of these Old Republicans, whom northerners sometimes described as luxurious proprietors supported by the labor of slaves.

Linked with their opposition to restrictions upon commerce was the hatred of the Old Republicans for the federally chartered Bank of the United States. Their opposition (or, at least, that of many of them) was not limited to that great institution; they disliked the state banks, as well. There was nothing fundamentally ridiculous in their position. They were opposed to borrowing and debt; they were advocates of a simple agricultural economy; they were "hard-money men"; and the states, or the colonies, had prospered earlier without banks. Had they been able to perpetuate the society they loved, banks might not have been a necessity, though they might have been a convenience. But many of the Old Republicans thought such convenience outweighed by the evils of concentration of economic power, complication of the economy, and encouragement to extravagance the banks brought with them. The federal Bank was unconstitutional, moreover, they contended; and, in time, the people were to accept the latter contention of the Old Republicans.

Randolph wrote to Brockenbrough, president of the Bank of Virginia, that a banking house was a house of ill fame.[35] He saw the Bank of the United States as an unconstitutional monster, created for the benefit of an avaricious class and serving as a tool of the centralizers. His chief assault on the Bank came in 1816, during the debate over rechartering the institution. Randolph agreed that the circulating currency of the day was in a deplorable state of fluctuation, but he saw no remedy in the Bank—and, most certainly, no remedy worthy of the price that would have to be paid. True payments never can be made solely by credit and paper; precious metals, or paper bottomed on them, are indispensable. He foresaw a consequent management of the national economy by the federal executive to suit the will and discretion of politicians. The banks had become so powerful, such an influence upon almost all men of consequence, that "we are tied hand and foot to this great Mammon, which is set up to worship in this Christian land"; and the government, while denouncing religious hierarchy, establishes a new economic hierarchy:

> The stuff uttered on all hands, and absolutely got by rote by the haberdashers' boys behind the counters in the shops, [is] that paper now in circulation would buy anything you want as well as gold and silver....

He despaired, he said, almost of remedying the evil when he saw so many men of respectability directors, stockholders, debtors of the banks. To pass this bill, he said, would be like getting rid of the rats by setting fire to the house; whether any other remedy could be devised, he did not now undertake to pronounce. The banks, he said, had lost all shame, and exemplified a beautiful and very just observation of one of the finest writers, that men banded together in a common cause, will collectively do that at which every individual of the combination would spurn.[36]

And Randolph declared, several days later, that he was

the holder of no stock whatever, except live stock, and had determined never to own any; but if this bill passed, he would not only be a stockholder to the utmost of his power, but would advise every man, over whom he had any influence, to do the same, because it was the creation of a great privileged order of the most hateful kind to his feelings, and because he would rather be the master than the slave. If he must have a master, let him be one with epaulettes, something that he could fear and respect, something that he could look up to—but not a master with a quill behind his ear.[37]

The Bank was chartered; but Randolph was to triumph in death, for Jackson, whom he first supported and then cursed, carried on, in this respect at least, the Old Republican tradition. Nevertheless, time has brought the complicated credit economy Randolph dreaded, with finance the master of man. "Who can bind posterity?" Randolph exclaimed despairingly.

*〰 5 〰*

As early as 1811, John Randolph said of the Republicans of true principles:

# Randolph of Roanoke

He feared, if a writ were to issue against that old party—as had been
facetiously said of another body, of our valiant Army—it would be found
impossible for a constable with a search warrant to find it. There must
be a return *non est inventus*. Death, resignation, and desertion, had
thinned their ranks. They had disappeared. New men and new doctrines
had succeeded.[38]

The Republican principles of 1800 were indeed deserted by
most of their champions, out of necessity or inclination; but
Randolph and his allies were constant. Right or wrong, they
were faithful, and such fidelity in politics merits a high reward
which the Old Republicans never did receive. True, their principles coincided with the measures which would best protect
their class, and in that they may be said to have yielded to self-
interest; but Randolph, with his abhorrence of natural-rights
doctrine, would have admitted freely the impeachment. He
sought to safeguard himself and his society; that, and not abstract theory, he would have maintained, was the whole basis
of politics. Randolph and his friends fought for the agricultural
life. They were vanquished.

Yet those doctrines of 1800 did not perish; they were guarded,
battered but obdurate, by the Old Jacobins and were passed on
to a later generation of southern thought (and, in a measure,
of northern thought) which gave them a more hearty welcome
than they had long experienced. Those principles of a society
of freeholders have in them an attraction for some natures
which does not perish with the times. Those political standards,
in part the product and in part the corollary of this school of
thought, have been sorely trampled, but they have not been
refuted. Purity and economy in government, peace and prudence in foreign relations, and freedom from economic oppression by special interests are ideals which, if remote of achieve-
ment, still are worth striving toward.

## CHAPTER SIX

# *The Cancer*

GEORGE MASON, one of the three Virginians most admired by John Randolph, declared: "Every master of slaves is born a petty tyrant. They bring the judgment of heaven on a country."[1] Jefferson, Randolph's kinsman, attacked slavery as a deprivation of the divine gift of liberty, and added, "Indeed I tremble for my country when I reflect that God is just; that his justice cannot sleep forever."[2] And St. George Tucker, stepfather of Randolph, wrote his admirable *Dissertation on Slavery,* prefaced by the words of Montesquieu: "Slavery not only violates the laws of nature, and of civil society, but also wounds the best Forms of Government: in a Democracy, where all Men are equal, Slavery is contrary to the spirit of the Constitution."[3]

A half-century later, Calhoun, who considered himself the heir of Jefferson—and so he was, in many respects—said of slavery:

Be it good or bad, it has grown up with our society and institutions, and is so interwoven with them that to destroy it would be to destroy us as a people. But let me not be understood as admitting, even by implication, that the existing relation between the two races in the slaveholding States is an evil—far otherwise. I hold it to be a good, as it has thus far proved itself to be, to both, and will continue to prove so if not disturbed by the fell spirit of abolition.[4]

The bridge between these two schools of thought was John Randolph, the slaveholding *ami des noirs,* and possibly he faced reality more clearly than did his predecessors or his inheritors. On the question of slavery, more than any other single issue, the development of Randolph's thought is an index to the alteration of the southern mind during those years.

In his youth Randolph was a sturdy opponent of Negro slavery; he never ceased to deplore the institution; his consistency cannot be impeached; and yet, by the end of his life, his stand had become only a step removed from Calhoun's praise of servitude. In Randolph, too, the development of that dread of the Negro, emphasized by U. B. Phillips in his studies of the Old South, may be discerned clearly.

The problem of slavery, in its larger aspect, is closely bound to that of natural rights. As Randolph's degree of faith in natural rights is obscure during his early years, so is the precise extent of his earlier opposition to slavery. Henry Adams implies that Randolph was an ardent emancipator, literally the American *ami des noirs* he called himself, and quotes with some malice the Virginian's account of his boyhood: "brought up among Quakers, an ardent *ami des noirs,* to scuffle with negroes and overseers for something like a pittance of rent and profit upon my land and stock."[5] But to paint a Virginian of that day as an admirer of L'Ouverture, Dessalines, and Christophe, a fellow of Condorcet, Mirabeau, Pétion, and Gregoire, is a strain upon credulity; Randolph's use of the expression must be considered an example of his half-whimsical adoption of current political labels, just as he termed his Old Republicans "the old Jacobins enragés," though they were anything but literal Jacobins. The French program of racial fraternization could hardly have attracted Randolph. One might be an advocate of gradual abolition and yet not an equalitarian, and Randolph, in 1826, spoke of his youthful disgust with the institution:

From my early childhood, all my feelings and instincts were in opposition to slavery in every shape; to the subjugation of one man's will to that of another; and from the time that I read Clarkson's celebrated pamphlet, I was, I am afraid, as mad—as Clarkson himself. I read myself into this madness, as I have read myself into some agricultural improvements; but, as with these last, I worked myself out of them, so also I worked myself out of it.[6]

Although Randolph thus purged himself of what he considered the folly of governmental interference with slavery, he never altered his own humanitarian treatment of his hundreds of slaves. As a master, Randolph did indeed prove himself a friend of the blacks. The childless man of Roanoke, embittered against his era, treated his slaves with paternal pity and kindness, tempered by the necessity of keeping them in a proper awe. Powhatan Boulding tells us that Randolph, with his glittering eye, was held in awe by every Negro of the neighborhood;[7] but he was loved by them, also. The younger Josiah Quincy, an earnest advocate of emancipation, related this incident of Randolph's return to Roanoke, where he was met by his slaves: "Men and women rushed toward him, seized him by the hand with perfect familiarity, and burst into tears of delight at his presence among them. His conduct to these humble dependents was like that of a most affectionate father among his children."[8]

In his letters he frequently refers to his slaves as if they were friends or kinsmen. From London, in 1830, he wrote to William Leigh, referring to his two favorite household servants, "Before this Juba is at home. . . . Johnny was delighted to hear from home & sends his kind How D'ye? to all."[9] Johnny, who was with Randolph at the time of the Virginian's death in Philadelphia, had accompanied Randolph on his tours of Britain, and Randolph told Jacob Harvey, "Much as I was prepared to see misery in the South of Ireland, I was utterly shocked at the condition of the poor peasantry between Limerick and Dublin. Why, sir, John never felt so proud of being a *Virginia slave.* He looked with horror upon the mud hovels and miserable food of the *white slaves,* and I had no fear of *his* running away."[10] On the same trip, Randolph informed some Irish gentlemen that "if any of you should visit old Virginia, I shall promise you a fair hearing, at all events; and you may compare *our* system of slavery with yours—aye, and be the judges yourselves!"[11]

A conscientious master of fields and slaves in declining Virginia after the embargo and 1812 might very well be hard pressed to keep his Negroes properly fed and clothed; and a patriarchal proprietor like Randolph, who looked upon his slaves more as wards than as a source of income, had reason to inveigh against the original introduction of slavery, no matter how difficult it might be to remedy the evil now. After the devastating flood of the Roanoke in 1814, Randolph wrote to Brockenbrough: "With a family of more than two hundred mouths looking up to me for food, I feel an awful charge on my hands. It is easy to rid myself of the burthen if I could shut my heart to the cry of humanity and the voice of duty. But in these poor slaves I have found my best and most faithful friends; and I feel that it would be more difficult to abandon them to the cruel fate to which our laws would consign them, than to suffer with them."[12] Even the rogues among his blacks seemed like children to him; writing to an overseer of Benjamin Watkins Leigh's plantation, he remarked: "I send you a hand in lieu of Bull's (Moses') wife who had parted from him because he has deserted her and taken up with other women. His name is Davy. He is a sheep stealer and a hog stealer. Have an eye upon him. He is weak breasted, predisposed to Consumption. You must therefore not put him to any *hard* work or expose him to wet or cold."[13]

Such was the master who was the South's foremost opponent of federal interference with slavery. More like a baron among his peasants than a slaveowning entrepreneur of the Deep South, he never wavered in his hatred of the slave trade and never bought or sold slaves, no matter how great his immediate need for money might be. If he had ever wished to emancipate his slaves during his lifetime, he could not have done so, for they were included in the mortgage upon the Randolph estates which his father had given British creditors.[14] But the failure of the settlement at Israel Hill, where his brother Richard had established his own emancipated Negroes, probably would have deterred Randolph from hoping to set up his blacks as freedmen in the South; what provision he made in his will, we shall say a trifle about presently. At any rate, he was the terror of slave-traders, and the abolitionist Whittier was accurate when, in "Randolph of Roanoke," he praised the dead Virginian:

> He held his slaves, yet kept the while
> His reverence for the Human;
> In the dark vassals of his will
> He saw but Man and Woman.
> No hunter of God's outraged poor
> His Roanoke valley entered;
> No trader in the souls of men
> Across his threshold ventured.[15]

Though Randolph was no literal *ami des noirs,* he certainly was a southern friend to the Negroes in his own conduct. What his attitude became in public life is a more important question.

## 2

John Randolph had been a member of the House of Representatives only a year when a number of free blacks presented a petition requesting revision of the slave-trade laws and the fugitive-slave regulations, as well as the inception of a program of general emancipation. His stand on the matter was the beginning of his uncompromising defense of the right of the South to be free from external interference with her peculiar institution. He hoped that the House would act so decidedly in the negative as to deter petitioners from ever presenting a similar appeal. "The Constitution had put it out of the power of the House to do anything in it, and therefore he hoped the motion for a reference would be lost by a decided majority, and this would be the last time the business of the House would be entered upon, and the interest and feelings of the Southern States be put in jeopardy, by similar applications."[16] At this time Randolph ruled the House literally booted and spurred, the master of the new Republican Congress as much from terror as from love, and congressmen hastened to obey his edict: the House passed, eighty-five to one, a resolution declaring the parts of the petition referring to emancipation "have a tendency to create disquiet and jealousy, and ought therefore to receive no encouragement."[17] Randolph, with his accustomed prescience, had foreseen the probable consequence of such agitation, and for a long time he had squelched it. But, four decades later, similar petitions were to split the House into vituperative northern and southern camps.

During Randolph's second year in Congress occurred Gabriel's insurrection, the first of those servile rebellions which were to influence southern emotions so profoundly and, in the long run, to reinforce Randolph's plea for state rights and strict construction. At Bizarre, Randolph wrote to Nicholson, in Maryland, concerning the rising: "The accused have exhibited a spirit, which, if it becomes general, must deluge the Southern country with blood. They manifested a sense of their rights, and a thirst for revenge, which portend the most unhappy consequences."[18] Whether the phrase "a sense of their rights" indicated a recognition of natural rights possessed by slaves, it is hard to say. Less than two years later, Randolph's opposition to slavery appears to have been still virulently strong. As the chairman of a committee of the House to consider a petition of the people of Ohio (among them William Henry Harrison the chief mover) for a temporary suspension of the prohibition of slavery under the Ordinance of 1787, Randolph wrote a report denying their request and condemning the institution. It is noteworthy that Randolph never disputed the power of Congress to prohibit slavery in the territories, or, for that matter, in the District of Columbia; Congress, he said, governed the territories as an empire, before they became states. His report follows:

That the rapid population of the State of Ohio sufficiently evinces, in the opinion of your committee, that the labor of slaves is not necessary to promote the growth and settlement of colonies in that region. That this labor, demonstrably the dearest of any, can only be employed to advantage in the cultivation of products more valuable than any known to that quarter of the United States: that the committee deem it highly dangerous and inexpedient to impair a provision wisely calculated to promote the happiness and prosperity of the Northwestern country, and to give strength and security to that extensive frontier. In the salutary operation of this sagacious and benevolent restraint, it is believed that the inhabitants of Indiana will, at no very distant day, find ample remuneration for a temporary privation of labor and emigration.[19]

And Randolph was opposed to slavery in the South, as well. He condemned South Carolina's reopening of the slave trade; to Littleton Waller Tazewell he wrote in 1804:

To her [South Carolina's] indelible disgrace she has legalized this abomination and all her rice & indigo & cotton is to be converted into slaves. The labor of the miserable negro is to procure fresh companions of his wretchedness. I tremble for the dreadful retribution which this horrid thirst for African blood, which the legislators of that state are base enough to feel & yet more base to avow, may bring upon us. But a few years past, & the opulent nabobs of St. Domingo looked down with disdain on the feeble splendor of the beggarly noble class of Europe. In less than five years, the cause of the wretches will be recruited by 200,000 native Africans. It behooves Virginia, in my opinion, to look to the consequences.[20]

The question of slavery was not raised again in Randolph's congressional career until 1806, during the debate on a proposal to prohibit the importation of slaves after 1807—a dispute excited principally by the Carolinian reopening of the foreign slave trade, which we have seen Randolph denounce above. Yet he was among the most vigorous opponents of the particular bill introduced, a surprising fact in view of his detestation of the traffic; but his opposition was based upon jealousy for state and individual rights and upon fear of the precedent that would be established. He objected to that provision in the bill which implied that, under the constitutional proviso for halting the foreign slave trade, a master might be forbidden by the federal government from taking his own slaves out of one state into another. This, Randolph declared, was interference not with the foreign slave traffic but with the relation between master and slave—a power the federal government never should possess. Representative Early, of Georgia, made a declaration which Randolph neither indorsed nor contested and which reflected the growing resentment south of Mason and Dixon's line at northern criticism: "A large majority of the people in the Southern States do not consider slavery as a crime. They do not believe it immoral to hold human flesh in bondage. Many deprecate slavery as an evil; as a political evil; but not as a crime."[21]

On February 19 Randolph spoke on the topic. The Senate had rejected a House amendment to the effect that the right of a slaveowner to transport his property from one state to another be specifically guaranteed; and Randolph declared that the House ought to stand firm on the amendment.

If the bill passed without the amendment, the Southern people would set the law at defiance. He would begin the example. He would go with his own slaves, and be at the expense of asserting the rights of slaveholders. The next step would be to prohibit the slaveholder himself going from one state to another. This bill, without the amendment, was worse than the exaction of ship money. The proprietor of sacred and chartered rights is prevented the Constitutional use of his property.[22]

Already the determination of southerners to "set at defiance" what it considered unconstitutional interference with its peculiar institution was manifest here. On February 26 Randolph spoke again, remarking that the bill, if passed, might provide precedent for some future scheme of universal emancipation. "It went to blow up the Constitution in ruins. Mr. R. said, if ever the time of disunion between the States should arrive, the line of severance would be between the slaveholding and the non-slaveholding States."[23] Representative Goldsborough defended the bill, and Randolph replied: "He considered it no imputation to be a slaveholder, more than to be born in a particular country. It was a thing with which they had no more to do than with their own procreation."[24]

Finally the bill passed in a form more satisfactory to Randolph, but the great issue had been opened to public view. Henceforth Randolph often was to refer defiantly to his fellow-congressmen from the South as "my fellow slaveholders," in reply to New England's reproaches. His prediction as to the "line of severance" was to prove fatally penetrating, although in 1806, with separatist movements in the West and in Massachusetts apparently more ominous, the nature of future disunion was hardly so obvious as it later became. And here we see the first instance of Randolph's deliberate utilization of southern fear for slavery to gain support for his state-rights principles—the aspect of Randolph's career which Henry Adams considers most important.[25] Randolph, the purist in politics, the St. Michael disappointed in men and measures, came to appeal most successfully to men's economic motives and vague dreads in order to raise bulwarks for the society he loved. He might himself oppose slavery, but he would not refuse the support of those who inclined toward the institution. From this date forward, Randolph appealed to the slaveowners of the South to stand by strict constitutional construction and state rights, or else their slave property must be at the mercy of the North—indeed, the whole security of white people in the South would be imperiled. This appeal carried weight which no other argument could have furnished; it sufficed to convert southern members of the National Republican faction, former Federalists in the South, and others given to centralizing and loose-construction tendencies.

Randolph's fear of the consequences arising from federal interference with slavery was quite genuine and strongly influenced his support of the doctrines of strict construction and state rights; but it was not the only motive, nor the most important motive with him, for he had been a champion of those causes before the question of congressional intervention in slavery assumed any prominence. He used it, however, as a rallying cry for the Old Republicans; and he utilized the issue of slavery to advance his views upon questions other than constitutional construction and local liberties. He appealed to the southern fear of black insurrection—a fear which he shared—to further his program of isolation from European quarrels. His next expression of opinion upon slavery and the South is found in his speech on foreign relations, December 9, 1811. The War Hawks, bitterly opposed by Randolph, had rendered almost inevitable a conflict with England, and Randolph made a last passionate appeal against the coming war. The recent and then continuing horrors in Haiti must have chilled many a southerner—Gabriel's insurrection was thought to have been inspired by the successful example of Santo Domingo—and the Southsider's skilful tongue dealt mercilessly with this delicate problem.

Mr. R. dwelt on the danger arising from the black population. He said he would touch this subject as tenderly as possible—it was with reluctance that he touched it at all—but in cases of great emergency, the State physician must not be deterred. . . . What was the situation of the slaveholding States? During the war of the Revolution, so fixed were their habits of subordination, that when the whole Southern country was overrun by the enemy, who invited them to desert, no fear was ever entertained of an insurrection of the slaves. . . . But should we therefore be unobservant spectators of the progress of society within the last twenty years—of the silent but powerful change wrought by time and chance, upon its composition and temper? When the fountains of the great deep of abomination were broken up, even the poor slaves had not escaped the general deluge. The French Revolution had polluted even them. Nay, there had not been wanting men in that House, witness their Legislative *Legendre,* the butcher who once held a seat there, to preach upon that floor these imprescriptible rights to a crowded audience of blacks in the galleries—teaching them that they are equal to their masters—in other words, advising them to cut their throats. Similar doctrines were dis-

# The Cancer

seminated by pedlers from New England and elsewhere, throughout the Southern country—and masters had been found so infatuated, as by their lives and conversation, by a general contempt of order, unthinkingly to cherish these seeds of self-destruction to them and their families. What was the consequence? Within the last ten years, repeated alarms of insurrection among the slaves—some of them awful indeed. From the spreading of this infernal doctrine, the whole Southern country had been thrown into a state of insecurity. Men dead to the operation of moral causes, had taken away from the poor slave his habits of loyalty and obedience to his master, which lightened his servitude by a double operation; beguiling his own cares and disarming his master's suspicions and severity; and now, like true empirics in politics, you are called upon to trust to the mere physical strength of the fetter which holds him in bondage. You have deprived him of all moral restraint, you have tempted him to eat of the fruit of knowledge, just enough to perfect him in wickedness; you have opened his eyes to his nakedness; you have armed his nature against the hand that has fed, that has clothed him, that has cherished him in sickness; that hand, which before he became a pupil of your school, he had been accustomed to press with respectful attention. You have done all this—and then show him the gibbet and the wheel, as incentives to a sullen, repugnant obedience. God forbid, sir, that the Southern States should ever see an enemy on their shores, with these infernal principles of French liberty in the van! While talking of Canada, some of us were shuddering for our own safety at home. He spoke from facts, when he said that the night-bell never tolled for fire in Richmond that the mother did not hug her infant more closely to her bosom.[26]

Such was not the speech of a literal *ami des noirs*. But it should not be thought that these eloquent injunctions against racial equality meant that Randolph was reconciled to slavery. Four years later he delivered a denunciation of the domestic slave trade that Garrison would not have hesitated to publish, recommending its abolition in the District of Columbia. Nowhere in the world, not even in Africa, he said, was there "so great and so infamous a slave market as in the metropolis, in the very Seat of Government of this nation, which prided itself on freedom." Randolph disavowed any intention of interfering with the delicate relation between slave and owner; but he would not endure a slave market, where were sold persons "bought either from cruel masters or kidnapped; and of those who were kidnapped ... there were two kinds—slaves stolen from their masters, and free persons stolen, as he might say, from themselves." He pointed out that recent economic developments in southern cultivation of cotton, tobacco, and especially sugar had increased the price of slaves, which provided temptation to "their base, hard-hearted masters" to sell "out of their families the negroes who had been raised among them." Washington ought to afford no countenance to inhumanity of this sort—"an assemblage of prisons where the unfortunate beings, reluctant, no doubt, to be torn from their connexions, and the affections of their lives, were incarcerated and chained down, and thence driven in fetters like beasts, to be paid for like cattle." Randoph moved that the Committee for the District of Columbia should be "instructed to inquire into the inhuman and illegal traffic in slaves carried on in the District, and to devise some speedy means to put a stop to it."[27]

But in a later Congress, Randolph criticized Cuthbert's proposal for establishing a registry of slaves on the ground that it might lead to unjustified federal interference in state and private affairs; he insisted that federal regulation of the slave traffic remain within constitutional bounds. "In exterminating the slave trade, Mr. R. said, he would join heart and hand with the gentleman from Georgia, if he chose, in carrying the war into the enemy's country, even into Africa, and endeavor to put it down there, so they did not go beyond the definite landmarks of the Constitution."[28]

Perhaps these speeches, delivered with Randolph's accustomed indifference to popularity, had some part in creating the doubt expressed by many as to the course Randolph would take when, in 1820, the Missouri question confronted Congress. Indeed, such southern misgivings as to Randolph's stand on federal interference with slavery are hardly explicable otherwise. The Old Republican, so detested during the war with Britain, by 1820 was becoming more popular than ever he had been since his break with Jefferson; events had begun to convince Virginia and the South of Randolph's foresight; Jefferson was bestirring himself against loose construction of the Constitution; and letters were beginning to appear in the *Richmond Enquirer* commending the master of Roanoke. Only Randolph's confirmed dislike for slavery and his apparent consent to allow Congress power to interfere with the institution in the territories could have induced anyone to think that Randolph might not stand for the freedom of Missouri to determine her own laws. A friend informed Randolph of these popular misgivings and wrote to Ritchie of the *Enquirer* that Randolph "expressed his astonishment, that a doubt could arise in the mind of anyone who has observed his course. He disclaimed all intention of abandoning state rights, much less the right of the people to *self-government.*"[29]

Of what Randolph said during the first Missouri debate, we know little, although references to his remarks by other congressmen show that he must have made one of his greatest speeches; he had quarreled, not long before, with the editors of the *National Intelligencer* and had demanded their expulsion from the House, so their omission of his address may have been intentional. He appears to have said little concerning slavery itself but to have discussed the constitutional rights of states—with him, the real question at issue. On February 26, 1820, he spoke four hours on the matter; we know the substance of his remarks only by hearsay. On March 1 he made a second oration, dealing with constitutional aspects of the Compromise. After the debate was done, Randolph wrote to Rutledge: "The Slaveholding interest has been sacrificed by Southern & Western men from slave-holding States, who have wanted to curry favor for very obvious purposes. . . . Your Mr. Lowndes, Mr. Speaker, Barbour of the Senate (a mere bladder of wind) & some other would-be Leaders who want also to curry favor for the same reasons (these I need not specify) are the true fathers of the compromise."[30]

Calhoun had voted for the Compromise then; but eighteen years later he paid this tribute to John Randolph:

He now believed that it was a dangerous measure, and that had it been met with such uncompromising zeal as a then distinguished and sagacious member from Virginia, now no more, opposed to it, abolition might have been crushed forever in its birth. He then thought of Mr. Randolph, as, he doubts not, many think of him now, who have not looked into this subject, that he was too unyielding, too uncompromising, to impracticable; but he had been taught his error, and took pleasure in acknowledging it.[31]

In the second Missouri debate, Randolph's stand against federal interference with the institutions of particular states was unaltered, but we have only one sentence in which he referred to the blacks: "I do now appeal to the nation, said he, whether this pretended sympathy for the rights of free negroes and mulattoes is to supercede the rights of the free white citizens, of ten times their whole number."[32] Such comparative silence on the slavery question could not endure long, however; the threat to slavery within the South was becoming too distinct for equivocation, and the centralizing tendencies of the general government again provoked Randolph's appeal to the fears of his fellow-slaveholders. In the debate of January, 1824, on internal improvements, he delivered what Henry Adams considers his greatest speech. After remarking the danger of loose construction with reference to the project for internal improvements, he added:

If Congress possesses the power to do what is proposed in this bill, they may not only enact a sedition law,—for there is precedent,—but they may emancipate every slave in the United States, and with stronger color of reason than they can exercise the power now contended for. And where will they find the power? They may follow the example of the gentleman who preceded me, and hook the power on to the first loop they find in the Constitution. They might take the preamble, perhaps the war-making power; or they might take a greater sweep, and say, with some gentlemen, that it is not to be found in this or that of the granted powers, but results from all of them, which is not only a dangerous but *the most* dangerous doctrine. Was it not demonstrable, Mr. R. asked, that slave labor is the dearest in the world, and that the existence of a large body of slaves is a source of danger? Suppose we are at war with a foreign power, and freedom should be offered them by Congress as an inducement to them to take a part in it; or suppose the country not at war, at every turn of this federal machine, at every successive census, that interest will find itself governed by another and increasing power, which is bound to it neither by the common tie of interest or feeling. And if ever the time shall arrive, as assuredly it has arrived elsewhere, and in all probability may arrive here, that a coalition of knavery and fanaticism shall, for any purpose, be got up on this floor, I ask gentlemen, who stand in the same predicament as I do, to look well to what they are now doing—to the colossal power with which they are now arming this government. The power to do what I allude to is, I aver, more honestly inferable from the war-making power than the power we are now about to exercise. Let them look forward to the time when such a question shall arise.[33]

Many thought Randolph's assertions exaggerated, but none of his prophecies was to prove more accurate than this. In the next decade John Quincy Adams was to threaten the South that the war power was the power of emancipation; and four decades later the prophecy would become the Emancipation Proclamation. This question would not down, nor would Randolph allow his fellow-legislators to forget it; he was carrying the war into Africa, as Calhoun later was to do; in part, he raised the slavery controversy because of his own fears on the subject and in some degree as a tool to gain southern support for his general political ideas. During the same month he forced the subject into a debate on the Greek problem. Webster had announced that one reason for intimidating Turkey was that Moslems held slaves. But what did our Constitution say about slavery? Randolph inquired.

Sir, I am not going to discuss the abstract question of liberty, or slavery, or any other abstract question. I go for matters of fact. But I would ask gentlemen in this House, who have the misfortune to reside on the wrong side of a certain mysterious parallel of latitude, to take this question seriously into consideration—whether the Government of the United States is prepared to say, that the act of holding human beings as property, is sufficient to place the party so offending under the ban of its high and mighty displeasure?[34]

Three months later the issue appeared in his speech on the tariff; for the tariff would impose dreadful privations upon the slaves, he said, depriving them of their annual blankets and their woolen suits. "It was notorious that the profits of slave labor had been, for a long time, on the decrease, and that, on a fair average, it scarcely reimbursed the expense of the slave, including the helpless ones, whether from infancy or age." The new tariff seemed calculated to produce emancipation by the curious method that "in case the slave shall not elope from his master, his master will run away from him." Such deliberate impoverishment of the South would be pushed further, Randolph predicted, as reapportionment of the House gave the North a dependable majority. Slave labor, he added in a note appended to this speech, was ruinously expensive, and Virginia would have been far more prosperous, and free from the humiliation of being dominated by the North, if she had sent all her blacks northward across the Ohio, in 1785, instead of ceding her northwest territory to Congress.[35]

Randolph's vehemence was redoubled in his speech of March, 1826, denouncing the proposed Panama Mission. Never did he turn the problem of slavery more deftly to general political purposes. That he fully felt the fears which he expressed is proved by his letters to friends, but he had also the purpose of dissuading Congress from embarking upon a program of intervention in Latin America. "You can no more make liberty out of Spanish matter than you can make a seventy-four out of a bundle of pine saplings," he had said. The Spanish-Americans had liberated their blacks. Could the United States join in friendship and alliance with such revolutionaries? He introduced a resolution requiring the President to lay before the Senate information concerning the emancipation program in Spanish America, and he followed this proposal with one of his most impassioned speeches. As with so many of his orations, it is real pain to chop it into excerpts, but it is too long for inclusion here. He discussed slavery at length. The revolutionists threatened Cuba, he said; once in Cuba, they would menace the United States with servile insurrection.

Sir, I know there are gentlemen, not only from the Northern, but from the Southern States, who think that this unhappy question—for such it is—of negro slavery—which the Constitution has vainly attempted to blink, by not using the term—should never be brought into public notice, more especially into that of Congress, and most especially, here. Sir, with every due respect for the gentlemen who think so, I differ from them *toto caelo*. Sir, it is a thing which cannot be hid—it is not a dry rot that you can cover with your carpet, until the house tumbles about your ears—you might as well try to hide in a volcano in full operation—it cannot he hid—it is a cancer in your face, and must be treated *secundum artem;* it must not be tampered with by quacks, who never saw the disease or the patient, and prescribe across the Atlantic; it must be, if you will, let alone; but on this very principle of letting it alone, it is that I have brought in my resolution. . . . I know that on it depends the life's blood of the little ones, which are lying in their cradles, in happy ignorance of what is passing around them; and not the white ones only; for shall not we too kill?[36]

He traced the development of the English movement against the slave trade; he showed how gradually that Society, of which he had been a member, became a society for abolition of slavery itself; he blamed Wilberforce, Stephen, and Zachary Macaulay for the alteration. Their benevolence had become madness. "Fanaticism, political or religious, has no stopping place short of Heaven—or Hell." These insensate idealists had come to love the blacks of Jamaica, Haiti, and Sierra Leone more than their own countrymen. These fanatics were devoted to the universal extirpation of slavery; they were not content to let a dying institution sink naturally into oblivion. Randolph foresaw that the English abolitionist movement would spread to America—as, of course, it did by the time of Van Buren's administration. The states must be awakened to the danger and must begin to meet it at once. "But, no, sir, the politico-religious Quack, like the Quack in medicine, and in everything else, will hear of nothing but his nostrum—all is to be forced—nothing can be trusted to time, or to nature." In the North, slavery already had run its course; it was senescent in Maryland, sick in Virginia's meadow and grain country (where no staple crop made slavery necessary or profitable), and doomed to decay with the lapse of time, elsewhere. Just as free-born Englishmen's ancestors once were serfs, just as the serfs of Russia and Poland were even now going through the transition to liberty, so would the operation of natural economic causes bring about the emancipation of American Negroes.

And shall we be made to suffer shipwreck, we of the South, in steering our bark through this *Euripus,* by the madness of our pilot and our own folly—steering between this Scylla and the Charybdis (not of the Bahama passage) but of the imprescriptible rights of Kings (*jure divino*) on the one hand, and the imprescriptible rights of Negro slaves on the other? Is there no medium? . . . I am contented to act the part of Cassandra, to lift up my voice, whether it will be heeded, or heard only to be disregarded, until too late.[37]

This was Randolph's last important congressional speech on the question of slavery—and his greatest. Langdon Cheves was to quote from it at the Nashville Convention in 1850.

That Randolph was genuinely alarmed at the danger of servile uprisings as a result of Latin-American influence is shown by a letter to William Leigh, in which he wrote of the Panama Mission scheme, "If the States and people of the Union can 'go' this, I predict the most awful consequences to the happiness of the country, and the security especially of the Southern and South-Western States."[38] It seems equally true, however, that he used the Panama question as an anvil on which to forge his weapons for use in the debates over constitutional construction and political isolation.

The Panama Mission proposal came to nothing, however; two years later Randolph left Congress forever, his hopes at least partially satisfied by the election of Jackson, and, after attending the Virginia Constitutional Convention, went to Russia as American minister. Augustus Foster, the British diplomat, thought Randolph "would have made an excellent Russian nobleman," and asserted that Randolph told him "slaves were necessary to form a gentleman."[39] Whatever the measure of accuracy in Foster's statements, the master of Roanoke, in defending the right of the South to settle her own problems, had not lost his old antipathy toward human bondage. In the year of the Panama debate, *Niles' Register* reported that Randolph declared: "I have no hesitation in saying slavery is a curse to the master. I have been held up, as any man will be, who speaks his mind fairly and boldly, as a blackish sort of a white and a whitish sort of a black—as an advocate for slavery in the abstract."[40] He told Josiah Quincy the younger that the greatest orator he had ever heard was a woman. "She was a slave. She was a mother, and her rostrum was the auction block." But, he added to Quincy, "we must concern ourselves with what is, and slavery exists. We must preserve the rights of the States, as guaranteed by the Constitution, or the negroes are at our throats. The question of slavery, as it is called, is to us a question of life and death. . . . You will find no instance in history where two distinct races have occupied the soil except in the relation of master and slave."[41]

These latter remarks are as good a summary of Randolph's views as can be found. To slavery he was opposed on principle all his life; but he saw it as a problem almost insoluble in the South, and he prepared, with increasing sternness, to wall it away from external interference. As he told the Virginia Convention, in 1829: "I have nothing to do with the consciences of men. The abolitionist is as free to hold his opinions as I am to hold mine—I do not find fault with him. I impute no demerit to him for them. But I will never suffer him to put a torch to my property, that he may slake it in the blood of all that are dear to me. I will arrest his hand if I can—by reason if I can—but if not, by force."[42]

In his last years this defensive policy led Randolph into expressions of intolerance on the subject foreign to his nature, and which would well serve those who seek to find in slavery the cause of the decline of liberalism in the South. This attitude of the last months of his life came, indeed, at a time when he was insane, according to the judgment of a court after his death; yet it is difficult to see in Randolph's insanity, here, anything but an exaggeration, provoked by tormenting disease and disappointment, of the conclusions toward which the southern mind was moving. Even in his madness, Randolph was prophetic of changing times and ways. One fearful slave rising had occurred during the inception of his career—Gabriel's revolt; another marked his last decline—Nat Turner's insurrection. To the debates in the Virginia legislature upon the question of gradual emancipation of the slaves, which followed the suppression of the Southampton rising, Randolph gave no encouragement; indeed, if we consider him to have been sane at the time, he would have taken drastic action to prevent any discussion of such a subject. Bolling told the legislature, in December, 1831: "Every intelligent individual admits that slavery is the most pernicious of all the evils with which the body politic can be afflicted. By none is this position denied, if we except the erratic John Randolph, who goes about like a troubled spirit, malignantly assaulting every individual against whom his spleen is excited." Only a few months before his death, Randolph, very much indeed like a troubled spirit, made his last speech to his constituents, at Charlotte Court House; he advocated the cause of South Carolina; he denounced the North, and grew angry at the fact that not long before a Negro preacher had spoken in a meeting-house in Charlotte, and warned of the dangers such racial equality brought with it; he then referred to the late insurrection and the debates in the legislature:

I am no prophet, but I then predicted the insurrection. The insurrection came; was ever such a panic? Dismay was spread throughout the country. I despised it when it was here. Look at the conduct of our last General Assembly. The speeches that were made there were little dreamed of.

## The Cancer

What kind of doctrine was preached on the floor of the House of Burgesses? If I had been there I should have moved that the first orator who took the liberty to advance that doctrine, should be arrested and prosecuted by the State's attorney.[43]

One might doubt the accuracy of the report of this speech, recorded only fragmentarily, were it not for a letter, scrawled in a feeble hand, which was written by Randolph nearly a year before he made this last address. It was the product of a dying man, provoked to an expression of passion by the course of the North and the centralizers; but it cannot be considered the letter of a man politically insane, for it recommended what was to be the sober policy of later southerners. There must be drudges in every state of society, Randolph wrote: "Take your choice of slaves or *nominal* free men. ... There is no equality that a liberal spirit will brook that is not composed of men equal to each other because elevated on the pedestal of slavery, or as rich Capitalists, Peers." Before the War of Independence, Virginia flourished, though her proportion of Negroes was much larger than at present. Virginia had *gentlemen,* then; now she would lack the spirit to oppose Great Britain in similar circumstances.

I look for civil war. You may live to see Winchester & Richmond in two different states. All south of the river will join S. Carolina & if the Rope of Sand miscalled the Fedl. Govt. does not take Cuba somebody else will do it. We have no choice. If England gets Havannah we are ruined. We *must* & *will* have it & then is vent for all our now unprofitable slaves. It will be a noble empire from Rappahannock to St. Jago de Cuba. Having Havannah & the Bay of Tampa, we can throttle the Mississippi & give law to the West.[44]

Here is the dream of William Walker forecast. The next day Randolph wrote to President Jackson in similar vein; to the very President of the United States he recommended immediate secession:

Let the fools and knaves in the two Houses of Congress disband and then strike at Cuba. It will give vent and profitable employment for all our now burthensome slaves. It will strengthen the *great slave holding interest.* We shall have at least every thing south of James River with

( 127 )

the naval depot at Norfolk. I say therefore, with Earl Grey, if the struggle does begin as I happen to know it will unless you avert it by a prompt redress of our intolerable wrongs, "I shall stand by my order." It is Slavery versus Anti-Slavery; and if the Fanatics and Fools in England drive matters over hard with Jamaica, she will be glad to throw herself under our protection. With the Havannah and the Bay of Tampa, the only port in the Gulf capable of receiving a first rate line of Battle Ship, we have a slip-knot around the throat of the Mississippi and we can strangle the Commerce of the *"Free* States" northwest of the river Ohio, if those States give us any annoyance. . . .

Nations, like men, can be governed only by *Interest;* and the Slave Interest has the knife at its throat in the hands of Fanatics and rogues and Fools and we *must* and *shall* and *will* defend ourselves. . . . Everything south of Ohio, except perhaps Kentucky and the Western District of Virginia, must be with us. With this noble country and Cuba, where we can make a hogshead of Sugar as easily as a pound can be grown on the Mississippi or in Florida, we shall have a vast empire capable of indefinite improvement and of supporting easily forty millions of people.[45]

The opinions of the *ami des noirs* in his last days, these. They might not have been his expressions had he been fully rational during those final months, but they indicate the way his thought was turning. Beverley Tucker, his half-brother and disciple, was to become one of the most ardent advocates of slavery; Calhoun, who listened to Randolph's Panama Mission speech, soon was to declare himself a supporter of the peculiar institution; and in Polk's administration a beginning was to be made in the contemplated program of expanding southward and westward the domain of slavery. The growing wrath of the Negro controversy had driven even the consistent Randolph into the position of advocating what he abhorred.

#### ༄ *3* ༄

One might expect of a statesman like Randolph, who was personally opposed to slavery but politically committed to the defense of the institution from external meddling, that he would seek an internal remedy. True, Jefferson and Mason, though they disapproved of bondage, did little enough to alter matters; and Randolph was too deeply involved in the attack on the centralizers and his own concerns to take much part in Virginian politics, but he was a member of the English society for suppression of the slave trade and for a time gave encouragement to the Colonization Society, as did John Taylor.[46] But he, like Taylor, seems to have hoped only for amelioration of the evil, not for its extirpation; and, with the increase of abolitionist activity in the North, he despaired of much improvement, condemning the foreign and domestic abolitionists for their ignorance. The course of his opinions is a gauge of southern reaction aaginstnorthern radicalism. He was willing to confess his hatred of slavery to northerners, and wrote to Josiah Quincy: "Like you, I feel a veneration for the place of my residence. . . . The curse of slavery, however,—an evil daily magnifying, great as it already is,—embitters many a moment of the Virginian landholder who is not duller than the clod beneath his feet."[47]

Before the American abolitionist movement became vigorous, Randolph's letters and remarks in Congress evince an admiration for Wilberforce and the other English opponents of the slave trade. "When I think on Wilberforce and his worthy compeers, I cannot despair. Ten such would have served Sodom."[48] In 1816 Randolph addressed a public meeting of the African Colonization Society in Washington, at which Henry Clay presided, and gave the organization his mild indorsement; thousands of slaveholders, he said, would manumit their slaves and, in consequence, of their cares, if a satisfactory place of refuge for the freedmen were provided.[49] This was the year of Randolph's speech against the District slave trade, cited previously. Two years later he again condemned that traffic and, indeed, all the abuses of slavery in a letter to Brockenbrough: "Avarice alone could have produced the slave-trade; avarice alone can drive, as it does drive, this infernal traffic, and the wretched victims of it, like so many post-horses, whipped to death in a mail-coach. Ambition has its reward in the pride, pomp, and circumstance of glorious war; but where are the trophies of avarice? the handcuff, the manacle, and the blood-stained cowhide? What man is worse received in society for being a hard master?"[50]

But Randolph grew cool toward projects for improving the lot of the Negro as the North grew warm in the Negro's cause and as the Missouri question loomed up. On February 24, 1820, during the time of the first Missouri debate, he wrote to Brock-enbrough, "These Yankees have almost reconciled me to negro slavery. They have produced a revulsion even on my mind, what then must the effect be on those who had no scruples on the subject?"[51] All the same, Randolph was not reconciled to slavery, as one learns from the will he had written in 1819 and which he rewrote in 1821 with substantially the same provisions. "I give my slaves," his first paragraph commences, "their freedom, to which my conscience tells me they are justly entitled. It has a long time been a matter of the deepest regret to me, that the circumstances under which I inherited them, and the obstacles thrown in the way by the laws of the land, have prevented my emancipating them in my lifetime, which it is my full intention to do, in case I can accomplish it."[52] Other paragraphs provided for the purchase of land outside Virginia on which to settle the freed slaves and for defraying their initial outlay. To have released his Negroes immediately and left them destitute in hostile Virginia—even had not law forbidden such action—would hardly have been kindness.

And as Randolph's general conservatism grew in intensity, so his suspicion of slavery-reform projects increased. As late as 1822 he was recognized abroad as a firm opponent of slavery, and upon his tour of England he spoke at the London meeting of the African Institution, accompanied to the hall by Wilberforce, Lord Calthorpe, Lord Lansdowne, Lord Nugent, and Henry Brougham—strange company for a slaveholder. Brougham praised Randolph's opposition to the slave trade, and Randolph himself declared, "He was impelled . . . to assure them that all that was exalted in station, in talent and in moral character among his countrymen was, as in England, firmly united for the suppression of this infamous traffic."[53] He continued to maintain an interest in the English movement after his return to America; but, as the course of affairs in the United States began to alter, Randolph broke with his British colleagues and attacked the African Colonization Society. "I am more and more set against all new things," he wrote to Brockenbrough, on January 30, 1826. "I am against all Colonization, &c., societies—am for the good old plan of making the negroes *work,* and thereby enabling the master to feed and clothe them well, and take care of them in sickness and old age."[54]

During the next month Randolph delivered the Panama Mission speech, in which he referred to the English reformers and the Colonization Society. They had first commenced as men professing to have no object but the abolition of the slave trade; by degrees, however, they had revealed another object, the doctrinaire abolition of slavery itself, regardless of circumstances and consequences. "I could name illustrious names that are laboring under delusion as strong as that which led away the French Convention, when they thought they were establishing liberty, equality, and fraternity, on a foundation slippery and red with human blood and judicial murder."[55] They should not be permitted to make the Southern States another Haiti. Freedom could not be granted immediately and unconditionally to the Negroes without terrible social consequences, equally injurious to either race; an ignorant, debased, and impoverished mass of people, deprived of the authority to which they had always looked for guidance, would ruin themselves and their former masters. Randolph may somewhat have exaggerated the violence of the probable consequences of general emancipation, as did almost all southerners; but the lamentable economic and social condition of most of the South ever since 1865 and the unhappy status of the Negro throughout America for the last eighty-five years are considerable vindication of Randolph's warnings against a hasty and indiscriminate application of positive law to a great social evil which could not be cured by mere legislation. Randolph and most later southern leaders— Rhett, for instance—seemed to have expected a deadly social or servile war in consequence of compulsory emancipation; and this, of course, never took place between southern whites and Negroes; but certainly the arbitrary forcing of a "solution" upon the South, after 1865, has produced violence, evasion, and economic vexations that do incalculable harm to southern society and character.

"Without meaning to say a word, at this time, against the Society, as an experiment, I must say it has failed; and, so far as it has done any thing, it has done mischief instead of good." With these words, Randolph of Roanoke severed his connection with the humanitarian societies. Their visionary solution could not be his. He had analyzed the problem of slavery and had offered what, perhaps, was the only satisfactory answer—to let time have its way. He anticipated Calhoun in arguing that two races cannot live together on equal terms; and our age has yet to solve that conundrum. He saw that foreign colonization of freed Negroes could not be even a palliative and perceived the only immediate hope for improving the condition of Negroes in amicable relations and joint endeavor by master and slave. Northern agitation made Randolph hate the abolitionist, but it never made him hate the Negro. Ultimately, Randolph declared, only the erasing force of time could moderate the evil; economic change would render slavery unprofitable anywhere in the South and, consequently, impossible to continue. Few men in the decades before the Civil War admitted the truth of that analysis, but its accuracy would be upheld by a great many modern students of history and political economy. Whether Randolph could ever have brought himself to approve of that inevitable solution is hard to determine; he hated bondage, but the old Virginian society he loved had many of its roots in servitude. He compared the gradual process of emancipation that would come to the gradual rise from serf-dom to liberty in England; but he hardly would have ap-proved of the racial intermingling which should accompany the parallel, although Randolph did not emphasize the racial inferiority of the African as Calhoun and his contemporaries were to do. This appeared to Randolph to be time's untying of the knot of slavery—unless fanaticism should sever it in Gor-dian fashion, the threat against which he warned the South.

Staving off that threat of interference from the North was too much even for the genius of Randolph. Dying, he stood by his libertarian principles, and with almost his last words con-firmed his grant of freedom and land to his "poor slaves." It must have given him grim satisfaction that he, the fierce de-fender of the slave states, should thus accomplish what the equalitarian Jefferson could not. "I always have believed that St. Thomas of Cantingbury's jewels were Bristol stones—in other words, that he was insolvent," he had written to Brocken-brough, years before. "What else could be expected from his gimcracks and crack-brained notions and 'improvements'?"

He died, and his freed blacks were sent to their lands in Ohio; there the people of an abolitionist state met them with violence and drove them from the farms the southern champion had purchased for them. The bitter humor of John Randolph would have been required to deal properly with this irony; and perhaps even his wit would have proved inadequate before the terrible solemnity that was the question of human bondage.

## CHAPTER SEVEN

# Change Is Not Reform

A GLOOMY statesman generally has been an anomaly in these United States. Pessimism and statecraft commonly are mutually exclusive, indeed. Similarly, truly conservative statesmen—leaders whose chief desire is the preservation of the ancient values of society—have been rare here; often men called conservatives have been eager for alteration of a nature calculated to encourage a very different kind of society—Hamilton most conspicuous among them. Professed devotion to the cause of undefined progress and innovation has been virtually a prerequisite for political advancement in this land of territorial and economic expansion. Clay, with his American System; Webster, with his sonorous nationalism—such names have lived. Calhoun, true enough, was both conservative and somber, but most men of a brooding character who obtained a temporary success in their day are almost forgotten now—witness Fisher Ames. John Randolph is one of the few conservative leaders this age has remembered, but he survives in the popular mind more for his eccentricities than for his statesmanship.

The idea of progress has so permeated modern American thought that one sometimes has difficulty convincing professors of history and politics that Randolph was a statesman at all. They ask, perhaps, that you give them an instance of some great constitutional change or social innovation which Randolph promoted; for, in their consciousness, "statesmanship" has come to imply political surgery, cutting at the organic structure of society. But Edmund Burke describes the statesman as possessing "a disposition to preserve and an ability to reform": the former talent takes precedence of the latter. This disposition to preserve was the ruling passion of Randolph's character. And his attempted reforms, his attacks upon political corruption, legislation for special interests, and the new industrial power, were all calculated to defend old ways against an ugly new order. Many a speech and phrase of Randolph's have a modern ring—not only by reason of the acuteness of his thought but for the clarity of his language, since he despised the floridity which even then was engulfing American oratory. But nothing of his has greater meaning for us than his remarks upon permanence and innovation, old against new. The concept of progress was absent from Randolph's political thought; he stood fast against change in federal and state constitutions, dreaded the West, and lamented the decay of the times and the men. Could he see our age, he would think his warnings vindicated.

Randolph said at the Virginia Convention, "This is a cardinal principle, that should govern all statesmen—never, without the strongest necessity, to disturb that which is at rest."[1] Probably no man ever has expressed more succinctly the conservative instinct. He spoke thus at the end of his life, but since the inception of his political career, almost his every action had found its motive in that thought. His most thorough and eloquent exposition of this idea came in 1829.

Such opinions as Randolph held never have been popular in this nation; but possibly they may be true. The origins of Randolph's conservatism can no more be determined precisely than can the prejudices of most men. His congenital antipathy toward cant had a part; the accident of birth which made him a great landholder had a part; but most important, probably, was Randolph's love for the life of old Virginia—the Virginia which had begun to fade away in Randolph's youth. That life must be protected and preserved, he declared; it was the best state of society he could see possible for Virginia and the nation, and he scoffed at striving for impossible perfection. His poetic imagination, which overleaped the obstacles ordinary politicians encountered, saw clearly the relation between political cause and social consequence: he knew that the life for which he struggled could not endure in an industrial civilization or in an equalitarian political system.

Yet Jefferson, too, was one of the planter-statesmen; and the liberalism of his mind contrasts most remarkably with the conservatism of Randolph's, the optimism of Monticello with the gloom of Roanoke. To Jefferson, John Adams wrote: "Your taste is judicious in liking better the dreams of the future than the history of the past."[2] For Randolph, the future was gray and the past resplendent. What accounts for this divergence of opinion? The difference between their ideals of the agricultural life had its share; Randolph's admiration of Burke contrasted with Jefferson's allegiance to the tradition of Locke; and, besides, perhaps Randolph, defeated, had not Jefferson's illusions. That persistent hopefulness of Jefferson's, that reluctance to adhere to any rigid standard, that very liberalism—willingness to experiment—of the author of the Declaration, made it difficult for him to accept the logic which Randolph expounded. Acceptance would have meant a partial sacrifice of the democratic principle, and that Jefferson could not have endured. Jefferson may have been the wiser in that he changed with times and saved at least a part of his American dream; but Randolph saw the issue bitterly clear, and he, who had expressed his wish to die like a gamecock in the pit, would yield to no man and no force.

*⚘ 2 ⚘*

Randolph the conservative statesman has three aspects: as a critic of men and manners; as an opponent of expansion; and as a foe of constitutional change. Randolph's significant observation as early as 1800, "I have a respect for all that is antique (with a few important exceptions)," hinted that what was for most Americans the age of public infancy was for Randolph the age of public decay; the "few exceptions" soon vanished from his system. America had no harsher critic of her failings.

Some may ascribe Randolph's despair to the irritations of his mental and physical constitution; but the matter seems to go far deeper than that, for he was joined in many of his complaints by men whose health was uninjured and whose minds always were lucid—Nathaniel Macon, for one, John Brockenbrough for another. Randolph spoke of the decline of morality in public affairs; and there was such decadence, perhaps inevitable as the enthusiasms of the Revolutionary era faded and as an expanding economy offered prizes to the unscrupulous. He described the decay of old Virginia—his *country,* he said—and he was accurate, for socially and economically Virginia did decay from the inception of the Jeffersonian embargo onward, and the Revolution had seriously weakened the planter of the old sort. Perhaps it is with Randolph that we discern the beginning of that tendency, later so general in the South even before the Civil War, to look back to a happier past.

The tongue of the Southside orator was terrible to malefactors, particularly to the Yazoo men; it could prevent, for a space, the rewarding of guilt; but it could not change the time. Randolph might be called St. Michael, but, though he possessed the archangel's wrath, he lacked his sword.

One observes in Randolph's reflections a deep discontent with the nation even during the first administration of Jefferson; and after he had broken with Jefferson's party upon the decency of the Yazoo affair, the morality of the abortive purchase of Florida, and the costly embargo—all, in part, questions of political conservatism against the spirit of the age—his disgust became despair. To George Hay he wrote, early in 1806: "The old Republican party is already ruined, past redemption. New men and new passions are the order of the day—except such of the first as have sunk into time servers, usurers, and money changers."[3]

And the country, too, was declining, said Randolph; his pathetic observations upon the decline of his Virginia commenced with the adoption of the embargo and were intensified by the ruinous effects of the War of 1812. To Josiah Quincy he wrote in March, 1814, that Tidewater Virginia was one desolate expanse of dismantled houses, ruinous churches, abandoned fields, mournful evergreens replacing the prosperous old countryside. The old families were gone, too, and their place taken by "the rich vulgar," sprung up from commerce and war profits. "These fellows will 'never get rid of Blackfriars'; and they make up in ostentation for their other deficiencies, of which they are always unconscious and sometimes ashamed."[4]

Here was the old Virginia planter with a vengeance, in high disdain for trade. An even more melancholy letter was sent to Quincy on July 1. Whatever prosperity remained in Virginia, Randolph observed, had retreated west of Petersburg, Richmond, and Alexandria and east of the mountains; the West was a wilderness, the Tidewater nearly deserted, though so well situated for commerce. Deer and wild turkeys had become more plentiful near Williamsburg than in Kentucky; bears and panthers had reappeared in the neighborhood of the Dragon and Dismal swamps. He looked back with regret to the Old Dominion:

Before the Revolution the lower country of Virginia, pierced for more than a hundred miles from the seaboard by numerous bold and navigable rivers, was inhabited by a race of planters, of English descent, who dwelt on their principal estates on the borders of those noble streams. The proprietors were generally well educated,—some of them at the best schools of the mother country, the rest at William and Mary, then a seminary of *learning,* under able classical masters. Their habitations and establishments, for the most part spacious and costly, in some instances displayed taste and elegance. They were the seats of hospitality. The possessors were gentlemen,—better-bred men were not to be found in the British dominions. As yet party spirit was not. This fruitful source of mischief had not

# Change Is Not Reform

then poisoned society. Every door was open to those who maintained the appearance of gentlemen. Each planter might be said, almost without exaggeration, to have a harbor at his door. . . .

Free living, the war, docking entails (by one sweeping act of Assembly), but chiefly the statute of distributions, undermined these old establishments. Bad agriculture, too, contributed its share. The soil of the country in question, except on the margin of the rivers, where it *was* excellent, is (originally) a light, generous loam upon a sand; once exhausted, it is *dead.* . . . The tide swamps—a mine of wealth in South Carolina—here produce only miasma. You will find some good thoughts on this head, and on the decay of our agriculture generally, in our friend J. T.'s whimsical but sensible work *"Arator."*

Unlike you, we had a *church* to pull down, and its destruction contributed to swell the general ruin. The temples of the living God were abandoned, the *glebe* sold, the University pillaged. The old mansions, where they have been spared by fire (the consequence of the poverty and carelessness of their present tenants), are fast falling to decay; the families, with a few exceptions, dispersed from St. Mary's to St. Louis; such as remain here sunk into obscurity. They whose fathers rode in coaches and drank the choicest wines now ride on saddlebags, and drink grog, when they can get it. What enterprise or capital there was in the country retired westward. . . .[5]

For Randolph, the forces behind this decay were in part the irresistible strength of time and nature, in part the failure of the men of his day, and in part the result of restrictive commercial policies enacted by Congress. He fought hard against all three. The next year, Randolph admitted gloomily of Virginia: "We are not only centuries behind our Northern neighbors, but at least 40 years behind ourselves."[6]

The nation was censured even more severely by Randolph. Of his frequent railings against the degeneracy of the time, perhaps the best is contained in his speech against the Bank bill, in 1816. "We deceive ourselves; we are almost in the day of Sylla and Marius; yes, we have almost got down to the times of Jugurtha." The spirit of avarice was corrupting the whole American people, so that "a man might as well go to Constantinople to preach against Christianity, as to get up here and preach against the Banks." He lamented that restless covetousness which Tocqueville found so strong a decade and a half later:

> The evil of the times is a spirit engendered in this republic, fatal to the republican principles—fatal to republican virtue: a spirit to live by any means but those of honest industry; a spirit of profusion: in other words, the spirit of Catiline himself—*alieni avidus sui profusus*—a spirit of expediency, not only in public but in private life; the system of Didler in the farce—living any way and well; wearing an expensive coat, and drinking the finest wines, at any body's expense. . . . If we mean to transmit our institutions unimpaired to posterity; if some, now living, wish to continue to live under the same institutions by which they are now ruled—and with all its evils, real or imaginary, I presume no man will question that we live under the easiest government on the globe—we must put bounds to the spirit which seeks wealth by every path but the plain and regular path of honest industry and honest fame.[7]

In this vein Randolph steadily denounced the deterioration of American character, especially in congressmen. Both the House and the Senate, he wrote to Gilmer, in 1821, "abound in men not merely without cultivation, (that was to be looked for), but in men of mean understandings, and meaner principles and manners."[8] These were not merely the complaints of a dreamer of ideal political purity, for even in his hopeful youth Randolph had recognized the limitations of men and governments. Party and faction, for instance, cannot be eliminated in any society, as he wrote to Monroe in 1803: "We rail at faction without reflecting that the remedy which, alone, can remove her, is worse than the disease. I speak of forms;—for madmen alone can expect to see a whole nation deterred from intrigue & calumny by mere moral considerations. Let us not, then, be so childish as to expect from government effects utterly inconsistent with it."[9] And the next year he told Tazewell that "cabal is the necessary effect of freedom. Where men are left free to act, we must calculate on their being governed by their interests and passions."[10] This is very like Burke. Character, said Randolph, was giving way because the simple society which had produced the grand old Virginian and American character was undermined by economic alteration and governmental tinkering. "But I am becoming censorious—and how can I help it, in this canting and speaking age, where the very children are made to cry or laugh as a well-drilled recruit shoulders or grounds his firelock."[11]

The white population of Virginia, the old amusements and holidays, the very inns, were sinking into a listless decrepitude. Randolph wrote to Brockenbrough, near the end of his life:

> On my road to Buckingham, I passed a night in Farmville, in an apartment which in England they would not have thought fit for my servant; nor on the continent did he ever occupy so mean a one. Wherever I stop, it is the same—walls black and filthy—bed and furniture sordid—furniture scanty and mean, generally broken—no mirror—no fire-irons—in short, dirt and discomfort universally prevail, and in most private houses the matter is not mended. . . . The old gentry are gone and the *nouveaux riche,* where they have the inclination, do not know how to live. . . . Poverty stalking through the land, while we are engaged in political metaphysics, and, amidst our filth and vermin, like the Spaniard and Portugese, look down with contempt on other nations, England and France especially. We hug our lousy cloaks around us, take another *chaw of tubbacker,* float the room with nastiness, or ruin the grate and fire-irons, where they happen not to be rusty, and try conclusions upon constitutional points.[12]

Neglecting the pleasures of simplicity and the satisfactions which honest work brings, the Americans were corrupted by a passion for tinkering with politics and the taxing power, Randolph often repeated. "It won't do for a man, who wishes to indulge in dreams of human dignity and worth, to pass thirty years in public life. . . . The country is ruined past redemption; it is ruined in the spirit and character of the people."[13] He told Jackson that he much preferred the permanence of English institutions to those of America, "where all is ceaseless and senseless change."[14] "In truth, we are a fussical and fudgical people. We do stand in need of 'Internal Improvement'—beginning in our own bosoms, extending to our families and plantations, or whatever our occupation may be; and the man that stays at home and minds his own business, is the one that is doing all that can be done (*rebus existentibus*) to mitigate the evils of the times."[15]

So much for Randolph's verdict upon American instability. He was one of the few statesmen who have been hostile critics of their whole society and yet have managed to retain a considerable political influence. Very probably John Randolph of Roanoke would have been a critic of any society in which he found himself; but the bedraggled equalitarianism of early nineteenth-century America drove him close to fury. He perceived in his day that corruption and perversion of republican institutions to private advantage which ever since have been so lamentably conspicuous a feature in our governmental system. He saw, clearly, the doom of his Virginia, and the causes of that doom. Perhaps he was wiser than Jefferson in his view of the laws of descent; for if Jefferson expected the abolition of entail to bring about the predominance of prosperous yeoman farmers in Virginia, he was disappointed; and Randolph discerned in that act, with truth, the ruin of many an old Virginian family. Randolph's analysis of the consequences of the American laws of inheritance is strikingly similar to that made by the political sagacity of Tocqueville. Of men and morals in his age, Randolph held an opinion thoroughly contemptuous; probably the sight of humanity in industrialized and standardized America, a century and a quarter later, would have left even Randolph speechless. Toward the end, he felt sure that what Tocqueville was to call "democratic despotism," the triumph of dull and intolerant mediocrity, could hardly be averted; one could not bind future generations, and he told Brockenbrough:

Of all the follies that man is prone to, that of thinking he can regulate the conduct of others, is the most inveterate and preposterous. . . . What has become of all the countless generations that have preceded us? Just what will become of us, and of our successors. Each will follow the devices and desires of its own heart, and very reasonably expect that its

## Change Is Not Reform

descendants will not, but will do, like good boys and girls, as they are bid. . . . If ever I undertake to educate, or regulate any matter, it shall be a thing that cannot talk. I have been a Quixotte in this matter, and well have I been rewarded—as well as the woful Knight among the galley slaves in the Brown mountain.[16]

≈ 3 ≈

Westward expansion always has been too popular a subject in America for many congressmen to offer opposition to the program. The Federalists and their inheritors, indeed, sometimes stood against western enthusiasm, avowedly or covertly; but a Republican planter, John Randolph, declared unequivocally that the West was a curse to the Union, not a blessing, and opposed the admission of any new states. This is the second principal distinction of Randolph as the champion of permanence against change.

It may seem strange that an advocate of the agricultural interest, like Randolph, should be foremost in opposition to the pioneer communities beyond the mountains; but his motives were numerous and weighty. Although the West was at first agricultural, it had no desire to remain in that condition and was hardly second to the manufacturing interests of the Middle Atlantic States in the demand for stimulation of domestic industries. Then, too, the West was the home of belligerent nationalism; thence came most of the War Hawks, "the Grundys, Clays, and Seavers," that Randolph hated.[17] Moreover, the West was the seat of radical equalitarianism, and the western state constitutions were anathema to Randolph. But most important was the fact that Randolph knew old constitutions and old ways could not survive in a vast federated—or centralized—empire stretching from Atlantic to Pacific; aside from the physical obstacles to true federal union, the Western States, with their arbitrarily determined boundaries, had not the tradition of local rights and local distinctiveness—the spirit of particularism—which made the old Union in truth the confederacy Ran-

( 143 )

dolph called it. Expansion meant nationalism or centralism and destruction of the confederate spirit. The interests of the West were opposed to those of the East, said Randolph, and their provinces would come to govern them. Randolph was a sectionalist or regionalist only out of political necessity and had little more love for sectional unity than for national unity; but the rise of the West was a blow at "the good old thirteen United States" of Randolph's phrase; and Randolph set his face against it.

Yet it was the western question which led Randolph into the only act of his political career which his hostile critics may with some justice term inconsistency: he was the champion, in the House, of Jefferson's Louisiana Purchase, and he defended both the expediency and the constitutionality of that measure. This was less an inconsistency than that on the tariff question charged against Calhoun, or that on the bank question charged against Clay. Randolph had not then broken with the Jeffersonian party; the danger of western domination of national policies was not then apparent; the possibility of general loose constitutional construction by the Republicans had not then appeared; and Randolph seems to have stood for the purchase more on the ground that it would remove a dangerous foreign neighbor—a part of his program of American aloofness from foreign quarrels—than as a matter of aggrandizement and manifest destiny.[18] Randolph never specifically recanted his declaration of the constitutionality of the purchase, but he freely admitted his error in recommending congressional approval of Jefferson's action, for, as he said later, that purchase had been a severe blow at constitutional precedent and at the older states of the Union. As early as 1805, Randolph proclaimed that, because of the precedent it had established, "the Louisiana purchase was the greatest curse that ever befel us."[19] His war against the West had commenced. Seventeen years later he said of the purchase:

He remembered well the predictions, the sad vaticinations, on the acquisition of Louisiana. . . . We were than called on, Mr. Randolph continued, by some of the very men who had a hand in framing the Constitution, and whose wisdom has been so loudly, and not unjustly, applauded, to pause before we signed that treaty, admitting vast regions of country into the Confederation. We were forewarned, but not fore-armed, said he, as we are now experiencing—what we are now beginning to experience, I repeat—for we are yet in the green tree; and, when the time comes when the whole country is filled up, if these things are now done in the green tree, what will be done in the dry? I, for one, although forewarned, was not forearmed. If I had been, I have no hesitation in declaring, that I would have said to the imperial Dejanira of modern times—take back your fatal present! I would have staked the free navi-gation of the Mississippi on the sword, and we must have gained it.[20]

In short, Randolph would have had the nation acquire the commercial advantages of the Mississippi by intimidation or by force, and not have incorporated, in the process, those vast areas which were to change the whole character of the United States. Only three years after the purchase, he was speaking con-temptuously of the "new-fangled country over the Mississippi" and beginning to call Kentucky "the Australia of Virginia." One of his most vigorous statements of his stand is to be found in a letter to that other—and Federalist—champion of the East, Josiah Quincy:

We are the first people that ever acquired provinces, either by conquest or purchase (Mr. Blackstone says they are the same), not for us to govern, but that they might *govern us,*—that we might be ruled to our ruin by people bound to us by no common tie of interest or sentiment. But such, whatever may be the incredulity of posterity, is the fact. Match it, if you can, in the savage laws of Lycurgus, or the brutal castes of Hindostan.[21]

The following year, Randolph wrote to Brockenbrough, "Louisiana is not my country. I respect as much the opinions of the people of London as of the Western States."[22] And yet Ran-dolph, with his prophet's vision, sensed that the struggle against the West was in vain and said as much to the northerners who, at the time of the Missouri debate, would have sought to exclude that state from the Union:

> I do look with a sentiment I cannot express, said Mr. R.—I look with a sentiment of pity—and that has been said to be nearly allied to love, as I know it to be allied to a very different emotion—I look with pity on those who believe, that, by their feeble efforts in this House, governed by forms and technicalities . . . they can stop the growth of the rising Empire in the West. Let gentlemen lay a resolution on the table, let it be engrossed by a fair hand, and do you, Mr. Speaker, sign it, that the waves of the Mississippi shall not seek the ocean, and then send your Sergeant-at-Arms to carry it into execution, and see whether you can enforce it with all the force, physical and moral, under your control.[23]

All the same, Randolph himself did not vote in favor of the admission of Missouri; although he vehemently opposed the terms proposed for Missouri by the antislavery faction, doubtless he was sorry to see any great new western state enter the Union. "No Government, extending from the Atlantic to the Pacific, can be fit to govern me or those whom I represent."[24] So he proclaimed in 1822; and in that same year he pointed out what a danger the West was to the preservation of the Union: the Missouri debate had been only the signpost indicating a series of such perils. He said of Virginia's generous early cession of her lands north of the Ohio to the nation, "By that act, the great river Ohio, in itself a natural limit—that natural limit is made (I speak in the spirit of foresight) the permanent and unfading line of future division, if not in the Government, in the councils, of the Country."[25]

And in his last great congressional speech, that on retrenchment and reform, in 1828, Randolph defended unflinchingly the course of opposition to the West he had long pursued. The new states had been vast deserts, rightfully belonging to the Indians. Although very dense populations, the rabble of great cities, are a terrible danger to good political institutions, barbaric lands scarcely settled are no less dangerous to social tranquillity. Most important of all, this giving inchoate and almost uninhabited regions a voice in the Senate equal to that of ancient and populous communities, possessed of traditions and property, was political stupidity and injustice:

> I have always said, and shall forever hold it to be the height of injustice (and of folly, too, on the part of the old States) that thirty or forty thousand persons, who so long as they remained in Pennsylvania or Virginia, were represented in the Senate, only as the rest of the Pennsylvanians and Virginians, should, by emigrating to one of the geographical diagrams beyond the Ohio or the Mississippi, acquire, *ipso facto,* an equipollent vote in the other House of Congress with the millions that they left behind at home. In case of the old States, necessity gave this privilege to Rhode Island, &c. . . .
>
> Sir, do not understand me as wishing to establish injurious or degrading distinctions between the old and the new states, to the disadvantage of these last. . . . No, sir, my objection was to the admission of such States (whether south or north of the Ohio, east or west of the Mississippi) into the Union, and by consequence, to a full participation of power in the Senate with the oldest and largest members of the confederacy, before they had acquired a sufficient population that might entitle them to it, and before that population had settled down into that degree of consistency and assimilation which is necessary to the formation of a body politic. . . . If I had been an emigrant myself to one of these new States—and I have near and dear connexions in some of them—I could not have murmured against the denial to forty or fifty thousand new settlers . . . of a voice in the Senate, potential as New York's, with a million and a half of people.[26]

In this defense by a man who boasted of never having voted for the admission of a new state we discern one of Randolph's primary political theories: that governmental questions should be determined not by abstract claims of natural equality but by enlightened expediency founded upon considerations of practicality and traditional experience. The western regions should not be admitted simply upon their claim to be independent and equal bodies of freemen; they must first show some physical equality, some equality of power, with the older states.

Such was the view Randolph's conservative mind took of the West. Randolph seems not to have hoped to have overcome the

West forever but only to have delayed the admission of new states until they could become states in truth. He was not wrong in his analysis of the nature of the West, whether or not one agrees with his conservative opposition. From the West came the radical constitutional ideas which swept back over the eastern region of Virginia in 1829; from the West came nationalism, jingoism, and equalitarianism, all of which came from the West were of a nature foreign to Randolph's planter philosophy. Randolph knew what he fought, and, although he failed, he did not relent. He was buried with face to the setting sun, tradition says, so that he might keep his sharp eyes on Henry Clay and the West.[27]

⚘ 4 ⚘

In Randolph's short sentence, "Change is not reform," spoken at the Virginia Convention of 1829, was epitomized the thought of the great Virginian free lance. Many a man of his day must have thought such a stand inexplicable, even more would think so today; for in the minds of most Americans, "change" has become synonymous with "progress," and progress has become the object of a sort of new deism; whole schools of philosophy and of educational thought have accepted mystic "progress" as their only goal, without attempt at definition of terms. But John Randolph of Roanoke had his ideal—the ideal of individual freedom, the freedom he thought best exemplified by the life of old Virginia—too clearly delineated in his imagination for him to be tempted into theories of "progress" and "co-operation for a higher freedom." His contention that change and progress are not one but sometimes mutually exclusive received scant consideration in an American vision of grandeur. He fought all major alterations in federal and state constitutions, not because he thought those constitutions perfect, but because he knew they would be replaced by worse;

( 148 )

and no conservative thinker has more cogently expressed his creed than, late in life, did Randolph.

Once only was Randolph the proponent of constitutional change; and that was during the period of the impeachment and trial of Justice Chase in 1805. He recommended, before that unsuccessful prosecution, a constitutional amendment providing for removal of federal judges by vote of Congress, but it never was passed by House or Senate. Randolph spoke contemptuously of the "go-cart of precedent" and held that constitutions faced "amendment or deterioration"[28] then. Unchecked judicial interpretation of the Constitution always was a sore spot with Randolph, for the decisions of his friend John Marshall did more injury to Randolph's Constitution than did Federalist or Republican congresses. But his recommendation of reconsideration of constitutional questions was not to become a permanent part of his thought, since the Old Republicans soon found they had more to lose than to gain by constitutional alteration. Still, Randolph did not possess the reverence for the federal Constitution that was John C. Calhoun's; the man who had seen "the poison under the wings" of the federal butterfly thought the Constitution hardly perfect. The preceding disorders, he said, had induced the framers of the Constitution "to have a King Stork substituted for King Log." The American Constitution, he wrote to Quincy, possessed the faults inherent in political systems which are "made" rather than slowly developed; it lacked at once the elasticity and the prescriptive veneration of governmental institutions that grow out of centuries of experience. "I see nothing of this in our system. I perceive only a bundle of theories (bottomed on a Utopian ideal of human excellence) and in practice a corruption the most sordid and revolting."[29] This statement of principles is significant of Randolph's affection for English political institutions; but, since no other federal constitution was to be had, Randolph became the most able and constant advocate of strict construction of this Constitution.

The American passion for enacting positive law to cover every possible exigency—which, in essence, is a question of constitutional nature—roused Randolph's contempt and despair. He declared himself, like Jefferson, averse to making the extreme medicine of the Constitution our daily food. "We see, about November," he told the House in 1816, "about the time the fog sets in, men enough assembled in the various Legislatures, General and State, to make a regiment; then the legislative maggot begins to bite; then exists the rage to make new and repeal old laws. I should not think we would find ourselves at all worse off if no law of a general nature had been passed by either General or State Governments for ten or twelve years last past."[30] Eight years later he expressed his futile wish that Congress had done nothing but talk—or, still better, had slept—for many years previous. "If I could once see a Congress meet and adjourn without passing any law whatever, I should hail it as one of the most acceptable of omens."[31]

Of all Randolph's expressions, in Congress, of opposition to governmental haste and tinkering and innovation, the best came in a speech of May, 1824:

> In all beneficial changes in the natural world, and the sentiment is illustrated by one of the most beautiful effusions of imagination and genius that I ever read—in all those changes, which are the work of an all-wise, all-seeing and superintending providence, as in the insensible gradation by which the infant but expands into manhood, and from manhood to senility; or if you will, to caducity itself,—you will find imperceptible changes; you cannot see the object move, but take your eyes from it for a while, and like the index of that clock, you can see that it has moved. The old proverb says, God works good, and always by degrees. The devil, on the other hand, is bent on mischief, and always in a hurry. *He* cannot stay; his object is mischief, which can best be effected suddenly, and he must be gone to work elsewhere. . . .[32]

It was at the Virginia Convention, in 1829, that the dying Randolph made his most eloquent defiance of the forces of innovation and experiment. He filled the role which Chancellor Kent played at the similar reforming constitutional convention in New York. Virginia, by 1829, remained one of the few states which possessed an old-style constitution—a constitution, that is, with special safeguards for property, with a limited franchise, with some remnant of the institutions that had been hers in Colonial times. Representation in the legislature was weighted heavily in favor of the old Tidewater counties. Randolph fought hard for the preservation of the old constitution; he struggled especially for retention of the county courts, of jury trial, and of freehold suffrage—all of them old institutions in the English tradition; he endeavored to prevent the insertion of a clause providing for future amendments, for the old constitution of Virginia, like North Carolina's, had not flaunted that "grin of death," as Randolph called it.

In Randolph's first speech at the convention, he defined the conditions under which he would consider reform advisable; and, analyzing the situation of Virginia, he found the state constitution in no need of alteration.

As long as I have had any fixed opinions, I have been in the habit of considering the Constitution of Virginia, under which I have lived for more than half a century, with all its faults and failings, and with all the objections which practical men—not theorists and visionary speculators, have urged or can urge against it, as the very best Constitution; not for Japan; not for China; not for New England; or for Old England; but for this, our ancient Commonwealth of Virginia.

But, I am not such a bigot as to be unwilling, under any circumstances, however imperious, to change the Constitution under which I was born, I may say, certainly under which I was brought up, and under which, I had hoped to be carried to my grave. My principles on that subject are these: the grievance must first be clearly specified, and fully proved; it must be vital, or rather, deadly in its effect; its magnitude must be such as will justify prudent and reasonable men in taking the always delicate, often dangerous step, of making innovations in their fundamental law; and the remedy proposed must be reasonable and adequate to the end in view. When the grievance shall have been made out, I hold him to be not a loyal subject, but a political bigot, who would refuse to apply the suitable remedy.

But, I will not submit my case to a political physician; come his diploma from whence it may; who would at once prescribe all the medicines in the Pharmacopoeia, not only for the disease I now have, but for all the diseases of every possible kind I might ever have in future. These are my principles, and I am willing to carry them out; for, I will not hold any principles which I may not fairly carry out in practice.

Judge, then, with what surprise and pain, I found that not one department of this Government—no, not one—was left untouched by the spirit of innovation; (for I cannot call it reform). . . . Many innovations are proposed to be made, without any one practical grievance having been even suggested, much less shown.

I have by experience learned that changes, even in the ordinary law of the land, do not always operate as the drawer of the bill, or the Legislative, body may have anticipated; and of all things in the world, a Government, whether ready made, to suit casual customers, or made to order, is the very last that operates as its framers intended. Governments are like revolutions: you may put them in motion, but I defy you to control them after they are *in* motion. . . .

Mr. Chairman, the wisest thing this body could do, would be to return to the people from whom they came, *re infecta*. I am very willing to lend my aid to any very small and moderate reforms, which I can be made to believe that this our ancient Government requires. But, far better would it be that they were never made, and that our Constitution remained unchangeable like that of Lycurgus, than that we should break in upon the main pillars of the edifice.[33]

In this speech, of which only a fragment is given here, Randolph's principle of determining particular cases by particular circumstances, not by abstract laws, is most noticeable. He spoke in similar vein some time later:

It has been better said, than I am capable of saying it, that the lust of innovation—for it is a lust—that is the proper term for an unlawful desire —this lust of innovation—this *rerum novarum lubido*—has been the death of all Republics. All men of sense, ought to guard and warn their neighbors against it. Sir, I have felt deep affliction—mortification—and humiliation, at seeing this venerable fabric of our Government treated with as little ceremony as a mouse in the receiver of a natural philosopher and experimenter. . . .

Recollect that change is not always amendment. Remember that you have to reconcile to new institutions the whole mass of those who are contented with what they have, and seek no change—and besides these, all the disappointed of the other class; and what possible chance is there that your new Constitution can be accepted?[34]

## Change Is Not Reform

Randolph's great speech against any provision for future amendment of the constitution they were framing came on December 30, 1829. He said, in part:

I have remarked since the commencement of our deliberations—and with no small surprise—a very great anxiety to provide for *futurity*. Gentlemen, for example, are not content with any present discussion of the Constitution, unless we always consent to prescribe for all time hereafter. I had always thought him the most skillful physician who, when called to a patient, relieved him of the existing malady, without undertaking to prescribe for such as he might by possibility endure thereafter. . . .

Dr. Franklin, who, in shrewdness, especially in all that related to domestic life, was never excelled, used to say, that two movings were equal to one fire. So to any people, two Constitutions are worse than a fire. And gentlemen, as if they were afraid that this besetting sin of Republican Governments, this *rerum novarum lubido,* (to use a very homely phase but one that comes pat to the purpose,) this *maggot* of innovation, would cease to bite, are here gravely making provision, that this Constitution, which we should consider as a remedy for all the ills of the body politic, may itself be amended or modified at any future time. Sir, I am against any such provision. I should as soon think of introducing into a marriage contract a provision for divorce; and thus poisoning the greatest blessing of mankind and its very source—at its fountain head. He has seen little and has reflected less, who does not know that "necessity" is the great, powerful, governing principle of affairs here. Sir, I am not going into that question which puzzled Pandemonium, the question of liberty and necessity, "Free will, fix'd fate, foreknowledge absolute"; but, I do contend, that necessity is one of the principal instruments of all the good that man enjoys.

The happiness of the connubial union itself depends greatly on necessity; and when you touch this, you touch the arch, the key-stone of the arch, on which the happiness and well-being of society is founded. . . .

Sir, what are we about? Have we not been the undoing of what the wiser heads—I must be permitted to say so—yes, sir, what the wiser heads of our ancestors did more than half a century ago? Can any one believe that we, by any amendments of ours—by any of our scribbling on that parchment—any amulet—any legerdemain—charm—abrecadabra—of ours, can prevent our sons from doing the same thing? this is, from doing as they please, just as we are doing what we please? It is impossible. Who can bind posterity? When I hear gentlemen talk of making a Constitution "for all time"—and introducing provisions into it, "for all time"—and yet see men here, that are older than the Constitution we are about to destroy . . . it reminds me of the truces and peaces in Europe. They always begin, "In the name of the most holy and undivided Trinity," and go on to declare, "there shall be perfect and perpetual peace and unity between the subject of such and such potentates, for all time to come"—and, in less than seven years, they are at war again. . . .

It would seem as if we were endeavouring—(God forbid that I should insinuate that such was the intention of any here)—as if we were endeavouring to corrupt the people at the fountain-head. Sir, the great opprobrium of popular Government, is its instability. It was this, it was this which made the people of our Anglo-Saxon stock cling with such pertinacity to an independent judiciary, as the only means they could find to resist this vice of popular Governments. By such a provision as this, we are now inviting, and in a manner prompting, the people, to be dissatisfied with their Government. Sir, there is no need of this. Dissatisfaction will come, soon enough. . . .

Sir, I see no wisdom in making this provision for future changes. You must give Governments time to operate on the people, and give the people time to become gradually assimilated to their institutions. Almost any thing is better than this state of perpetual uncertainty. A people may have the best form of Government that the wit of man ever devised; and yet, from its uncertainty alone, may, in effect, live under the worse Government in the world. Sir, how often must I repeat, that *change* is not *reform*. I am willing that this new Constitution shall stand as long as it is possible for it to stand, and that, believe me, is a very short time. Sir, it is vain to deny it. They may say what they please about the old Constitution—the defect is not there. It is not in the form of the old edifice, neither in the design nor the execution: it is in the *material;* it is in the people of Virginia. To my knowledge that people are changed from what they have been. The four hundred men who went out to David were in debt. The fellow-laborers of Catiline were *in debt*. And I defy you to show me a desperately indebted people anywhere, who can bear a regular sober Government. I throw the challenge to all who hear me. I say that the character of the good old Virginia planter—the man who owned from five to twenty slaves, or less, who lived by hard work, and who paid his debts, is passed away. A new order of things is come. The period has arrived of living by one's wits—of living by contracting debts that one cannot pay—and above all, of living by office-hunting. . . . I say, that in such a state of things, the old Constitution was too good for them, they could not bear it. No, sir, they could not bear a freehold suffrage and a property representation. I have always endeavoured to do the people justice—but I will not flatter them—I will not pander to their appetite for change. I will not agree to any rule of future apportionment, or to any provision for changes called amendments to the Constitution. They who love change—who delight in public confusion—who wish to feed the cauldron and make it bubble—may vote if they please for future changes. But by what spell—by what formula are you going to bind all the people to all future time? *Quis custodiet custodes?* The days of Lycurgus are gone by, when he could swear the people not to alter the Constitution until he should return—*animo non revertendi.* You may make what entries upon parchment you please. Give me a Constitution that will last for half a century—that is all I wish for. No Constitution that you can make will last for the one-half of half a century. Sir, I will stake anything short of my salvation, that those who are malcontent now will be more malcontent three years hence than they are at this day. I have no favors for this Constitution. I shall vote against its adoption, and I shall advise the people of my district to set their faces—aye—and their shoulders against it. But if we are to have it—let us not have it with its death warrant in its very face; with the *facies hypocratica*—the Sardonic grin of death upon its countenance.[35]

The man of Roanoke was vindicated in his prediction of a brief life for the constitution adopted (for it endured only from 1830 to 1850) and of the renewed opposition from those who had agitated for that very new constitution—for they were assailing the new document within the year. As for his remarks upon permanence and change, and the binding of posterity, comment is hardly necessary. If any truths be self-evident, these are, in the lucid expression Randolph gave to them. Here is a similarity to Jefferson's contention that each generation must form its own institutions; but, while the man of Monticello commended such a state of society, the man of Roanoke recognized it only to deplore it. Randolph's piercing beneath the mask of institutions to find in the morality of society the real flaw in political systems is strong evidence of his wisdom.

A few days later John Randolph uttered that remark which is the best expression of the conservative spirit.

Mr. Randolph said, that he should vote against the amendment, and that on a principle which he had learned before he came into public life; and by which he had been governed during the whole course of his life, that it was always unwise—yes—highly unwise, to disturb a thing that was at rest. This was a great cardinal principle that should govern all wise statesmen—never without the strongest necessity to disturb that which was at rest.[36]

With this maxim, and with that phrase he so often repeated at the Convention, "Change is not reform," we may leave Randolph. By 1832 he was writing: "The Country is ruined past redemption by political and religious factions bidding at the auction of popularity where every thing is '*knocked down*' to the *lowest bidder*."[37] He had fought the good fight for the old ways, but the sands were fast running out, and, as he was dying, so was the old life he loved.

⇜ 5 ⇝

A recent writer lists three principal tenets of our democratic creed: belief in a fundamental law (natural-rights theory); belief in the freedom of the individual; and belief in the "mission of America."[38] If we are to accept this analysis, we find John Randolph of Roanoke in agreement with only one of the chief doctrines in the body of American political sentiment—the championship of the rights of the individual. Surely no man could be more jealous of his liberty, more resentful of governmental intrusion upon his privileges, than was the great Southside Virginian; he accepted with all his heart the principle of devotion to liberty. But he rejected "Rights of Man" theories utterly and took his stand with Burke; he sneered at the "American mission," advocated in his day by his enemies, Clay, Webster, and John Quincy Adams; he placed his faith in old ways and old Virginia. Randolph was in scant accord with the political tendencies of his time, and those of our age would find still less favor with him. Yet to disagree with *demos* need not be to err; the consequences of such dissent may be unpleasant, but the dissenter can have the truth with him. Certainly Randolph's opinions upon "fundamental law" and "America's mission" have prevailed in the sense that they are widely accepted now by students of politics, who, indeed, sometimes go further than did Randolph, and declare that the desire for individual liberty, too, is vain—futile in this time of troubles, at least. Randolph, knowing what a world with the characteristics of ours would be like, fought doggedly to stave off its coming.

This, then, was the political thought of John Randolph, the greatest of the Old Republicans. He found the basis of authority not in "natural right," not in Nature and Nature's God, but in the Christian concept of ordination and subordination, power balanced by tradition; and he thought that authority best wielded by freeholders. He stood for the liberty of individuals, localities, and states and strove to maintain the division of power so as to guarantee such liberty; as a part of that endeavor and in accord with his belief that his position was historically sound, he maintained a strict interpretation of the federal Constitution. He, the planter-statesman, saw contentment for man in an agricultural life and fought all policies—the tariff, foreign wars and alliances, special privileges—which endangered that society. He perceived slavery, the greatest problem of his state and section and nation, to be a cancer; but he thought that radical remedies would be worse than the disease. He looked upon innovation as decadence, not progress. Such was his credo; he upheld it with the sternest consistency and devoted his tortured life to a vain battle in its defense.

Whatever the eccentricities of his private character, they did not affect his political beliefs; as Beverley Tucker wrote, "Many of his constituents seemed to think of him as the Mohammedans do of madmen—that in regard to politics he was inspired."[39] Perhaps nothing in American political philosophy is more brilliant than are Randolph's greatest speeches. "His political teaching never, of course, approached the dizzy mystic heights along which Burke alone could walk in safety," writes Keith Feiling of a great contemporary of Randolph, Canning;[40]

and the remark may be applied nearly as well to John Randolph. But Randolph was one of the very few American thinkers to realize that society is more than a contract for mutual convenience and to declare that political constitutions cannot be adjusted like clockwork.

Statesmanship is no uniform system; it is, instead, a patchwork concept. There are statesmen whose talent it is to manage, like Walpole; and statesmen whose talent it is to rebuild, like Sully; and statesmen whose talent it is to forge, like Cavour; and statesmen whose talent it is to criticize, like Burke. Randolph of Roanoke stands within the last category, of course; and acute self-criticism not being a virtue conspicuous in America, a man of Randolph's daring and penetration was required for the task of exposing American complacency after 1800. He was the sort of statesman who points out the natural boundaries of the state rather than the sort of statesman who is determined to enlarge those frontiers. After 1800 it seemed as if America was wholly convinced of her own omniscience—convinced that change was reform, that majorities were always just, that expansion was necessarily progress, that America could safely disregard the precepts of history and the formulas previously supposed to regulate society. America still believes in these generalizations, for the most part; but that these ideas never have been carried wholly to extremes, that our American complacency is leavened with a tiny, chastening grain of doubt —such limitations upon the reckless self-confidence of the United States are in part the contribution of Randolph and his colleagues.

Randolph's ideas spread throughout the South after 1820. The Missouri question, the tariff of 1824, congressional reapportionment, and presently nullification were the material causes of this alteration of the southern temper, of course, and it is hardly likely that Randolph could have revived the principles of the Old Republicans otherwise. But popular impulses cannot take coherent form without some system of ideas to arrange themselves upon, any more than ideas can achieve political consequences without the matter of popular impulse to sustain them; and Randolph's speeches provided that intellectual frame for southern alarm at the tariff, the slavery question, and consolidation. To Jefferson or John Taylor, with their eighteenth-century equalitarianism, the southerners of this new generation could hardly turn for guidance: the doctrine of majorities and the doctrine of natural equality both worked against the conservation of southern society. John Randolph, on the other hand, had outlined a political theory radically different, based upon the values of continuity and prescription, denying that rights exist in the abstract and that profound problems can be settled by the application of positive law. As the South became a conscious minority in the nation, southern leaders began to listen to Randolph with renewed interest, to reread his old speeches, and to imitate his uncompromising defiance.

When one leafs through yellow-old newspapers of the 1820's in the South, or blackens his fingers with the dust that lies upon the heavy volumes of *The Annals of Congress* and *The Register of Debates,* he becomes conscious of this southern revival of Randolph's influence, particularly after 1824. Resolutions are passed in southern towns and counties commending Randolph as the champion of state rights; he is quoted increasingly in Congress, as the years pass, and it is old John Randolph whose words Hayne quotes against Webster in 1830; his ideas and his methods are echoed in Washington and Richmond and Charleston. Oratory then retained an influence over American public opinion which, for the most part, it has since relinquished; and Randolph became the inspiration of that later school of southern orators whose efforts, all too often, were hardly better than burlesques of the nervous genius that Randolph possessed.

One indefatigable disseminator of Randolph's principles was Judge Nathaniel Beverley Tucker, of Missouri and Virginia, professor and novelist and southern sectionalist, Randolph's own half-brother. You see his grave close by the door of Bruton

Parish Church, in Williamsburg; in his day Tucker was aflame with resentment against the North, a fire which produced that curious novel *The Partisan Leader*. He did not let the South forget Randolph.

Other disciples of Randolph had begun as his adversaries—in particular, Langdon Cheves and John C. Calhoun. The aged Cheves invoked the shade of John Randolph at the Nashville Convention of 1850 in aid of his plea for immediate secession; thus the National Republican of 1811 had become the secessionist of four decades later. Calhoun's case is at once more important and more intricate. In earlier chapters, Calhoun's gradual conversion to Randolph's views has been touched upon. Although Calhoun to the end remained friendly toward American expansion, in almost all other respects he came to share the great Virginian orator's ideas. The tariff of 1824 revealed to Calhoun that nationalism was not synonymous with common interest; but the arguments furnished by Randolph lay ready to his hand, and Randolph's scintillating and discursive eloquence, which Calhoun could not imitate, made clear to the South Carolinian the real nature of that enormous controversy which until then he had discerned only vaguely.

"The man, the force that drove Calhoun into his realizations was none other than John Randolph," writes Calhoun's latest biographer, Margaret Coit. "For with all his vagaries, the Virginian was a realist. As early as 1816, he had seen through the 'tariff humbug,' long before bitter experience had brought a similar comprehension to Calhoun. All the throbbing, storm-tossed issues which were to torment the South and the nation for the next thirty years were passing before Randolph's tortured vision. . . . Calhoun listened."[41] Presently John C. Calhoun commenced that series of tributes to Randolph which runs through his later speeches and papers. In 1826, after Randolph's taunts in the Senate had provoked Clay to call him out—and had produced in consequence one of the most famous duels in American history—Vice-President Calhoun found it advisable to defend in the newspapers his own conduct as presiding officer of the Senate. "And who is Mr. Randolph?" he wrote. "Is he or his manners a stranger in our national councils? For more than a quarter of a century he has been a member of Congress, and during the whole time his character has remained unchanged. Highly talented, eloquent, severe, and eccentric; not unfrequently wandering from the question, but often uttering wisdom worthy of a Bacon, and wit that would not discredit a Sheridan, every Speaker had freely indulged him in his peculiar manner, and that without responsibility or censure."[42] This admiration presently became emulation. And, through Randolph's ideas, the spirit of Burke entered into Calhoun. So far as we can tell, Calhoun had read little of Burke; his references to the Whig genius are infrequent; but certainly a considerable part of that devotion to prudence and expedience, that contempt for abstract political ideals, and that suspicion of omnipotent majorities which we find in *A Disquisition on Government* seems to echo Burke. That Burke was not much more widely read, South and North, came to be a great pity.

In April, 1865, John S. Wise, a boy-officer who was a courier from the wreck of the Army of Northern Virginia to President Jefferson Davis, galloped by the desolate plantation of Roanoke, " 'Oh, John Randolph, John, John!' thought I, as I rode by, 'you have gotten some other Johns, in fact the whole breed of Johnnies, into a peck of trouble by the governmental notions which you left to them as a legacy.' "[43] No other man did so much, perhaps, to steel the resolution of the South. In 1837, replying to Webster, Calhoun had observed, "I regard it as one of the wisest maxims in human affairs, that when we see an inevitable evil, ... not to be resisted, approaching—to make concessions in time, when we can do it with dignity; and not to wait until necessity compels us to act, and when concession, instead of gratitude, will excite contempt. The maxim is not new. I have derived it from the greatest of modern statesmen, Edmund Burke."[44] Calhoun was speaking of the cession of the public lands to the several states, but of course his words apply with remarkable precision to those great issues which provoked the Civil War. That Randolph and Calhoun emulated the fiery determination of Burke more than they emulated his cautious "sounding the lead" is in some degree true; but, in the perspective of history, northern abstract humanitarianism and northern industrial selfishness are more guilty than these southerners of contempt for compromise and concession. With all the enduring evils it produced, the Civil War demonstrated at least one truth: that the power of government is not omnicompetent; that the alteration of social institutions is no mere automatic consequence of legislation; and that, when the government transcends certain bounds and threatens great interests and classes, it must be prepared to employ force, the negation of true government. Law has no right to tamper with the delicate social arrangements which only time can properly mend, Randolph and Calhoun declared. When government does usurp such powers, men will resist. The North never quite believed Randolph and Calhoun. The terror of the Civil War, the shameful years that followed—North and South—and much of the present sullen tone of American society are consequences.

The thirty-five years of Randolph's public career were spent in marking out the road which the South was to follow from the time of Jefferson to the time of Lincoln. From the Declaration of Independence to *A Discourse on the Constitution;* from the national democracy of 1800 to the southern nationalism of Yancey and Rhett; from *A Dissertation on Slavery* to Walker's filibusters and bloody Kansas; from the first tariff debate to Edmund Ruffin at his gun—this was to be the path. Had Randolph wholly foreseen the culmination, he might have been appalled, but he would not have flinched. For what else, he would have asked, could his Virginia and the South do? What else could men of honor do? They could not yield, and they could not triumph.

## Change Is Not Reform

In the southerners of the two generations that followed his, the Virginian patriot found his disciples, and their name was legion. And although Randolph's sovereign states have been beaten down at one time and bribed into submission at another; although every economic measure he denounced has been made a permanent policy of our national government; although the plantation is desolate and the city triumphant—still, Randolph's system of thought has its adherents. He has helped to insure us against reckless consolidation and arbitrary power. His love of personal and local liberties, his hatred of privilege, his perception of realities behind political metaphysics, his voice lifted against the god Whirl—these things endure.

When John Randolph of Roanoke was dying in a strange room in Philadelphia, he started up from his bed and cried out, "Remorse! Remorse!" As his life had tragedy strongly imprinted upon it, so had his death; but his remorse could not have been for his career in American politics. He had battled for principle against gods and men. And, though he fell, he lost with a brilliancy that was almost compensation for disaster.

# *Notes*

## CHAPTER ONE

### RANDOLPH AND HIS AGE

No collection of Randolph's speeches or correspondence exists. Randolph frequently complained of the inaccuracy of the reports of his speeches; and in cases where an error seems clearly to have been made, it has been amended in this book. In some cases the text of contemporary newspaper accounts is preferred to that of the *Annals of Congress*.

## CHAPTER TWO

### THE EDUCATION OF A REPUBLICAN

1. Henry Adams, *John Randolph*, chap. i.
2. V. L. Parrington, *The Romantic Revolution in America*, p. 9.
3. Henry Adams, *History of the United States*, IV, 107.
4. Randolph to Tucker, September 20, 1802 (John Randolph MSS, Duke University).
5. Hugh Garland, *Randolph of Roanoke*, I, 11.
6. *Ibid.*, p. 25.
7. *Ibid.*, p. 23.
8. *Ibid.*, p. 18.
9. R. T. Craighill, *The Virginia "Peerage,"* p. 290.
10. Randolph, *Letters of John Randolph to a Young Relative*, pp. 190–91.
11. H. B. Grigsby, *Discourse on Tazewell*, p. 14.
12. Grigsby, "Randolph's Library," *Southern Literary Messenger*, XX, 79.
13. Garland, *op. cit.*, II, 100.
14. *Ibid.*, pp. 9–10.
15. J. G. Baldwin, *Party Leaders*, p. 143.
16. Nathaniel Beverley Tucker, "Garland's Life of Randolph," *Southern Quarterly Review*, IV (new ser.; July, 1851), 41–46.
17. Josiah Quincy, *Figures of the Past*, p. 211.
18. Jacob Harvey, "Randolphiana," *Richmond Enquirer*, July 25, 1833.
19. Randolph to Rutledge, March 20, 1820 (Randolph MSS, Duke University).

20. R. B. Davis, *Francis Walker Gilmer,* p. 169.
21. William P. Trent, *Southern Statesmen of the Old Regime,* chap. iv.
22. Grigsby, "Randolph's Library," *op. cit.*
23. Richard Rush, *John Randolph at Home and Abroad,* p. 5.
24. Jacob Harvey, quoted by Garland, *op. cit.,* II, 175.
25. P. A. Bruce, *John Randolph* ("Library of Southern Literature," Vol. X), p. 4430.

## CHAPTER THREE

### The Basis of Authority

1. See H. V. S. Ogden, "The State of Nature and the Decline of Lockian Political Theory in England," *American Historical Review,* XLVI, 31–44.
2. John Dewey, *The Living Thoughts of Jefferson,* p. 6.
3. Gilbert Chinard, *Jefferson,* p. 87.
4. John Taylor, *Construction Construed,* p. 204.
5. Dumas Malone states that Thomas Cooper was the first southerner to express dissent from Jeffersonian theories; but Cooper's *Lectures on Political Economy* were published in 1828, years after Randolph had commenced his attacks (see Malone, *The Public Life of Cooper,* p. 290).
6. L. P. Namier, *England in the Age of the American Revolution,* p. 181.
7. Ogden, *op. cit.,* p. 27.
8. Edmund Burke, "Appeal from the New to the Old Whigs," *Works,* III, 85–86.
9. "Extract from a Private Letter," *Richmond Enquirer,* February 10, 1834.
10. Joseph G. Baldwin, *Party Leaders,* pp. 144–45.
11. Horace Gregory, "Our Writers and the Democratic Myth," *Bookman,* LXXV, 377–82.
12. Macon to Van Buren, May 24, 1836 (Macon Papers, North Carolina State Department of Archives and History).
13. Anonymous notes on Randolph (Nathan Loughborough MSS, copy in Randolph Papers, Virginia State Library).
14. *Annals of Congress* (9th Cong., 1st sess.), p. 562.
15. Randolph to Rutledge, April 29, 1797 (copy in Randolph Papers, Virginia State Library).
16. Randolph to Nicholson, August 12, 1800 (copy in Randolph Papers, Virginia State Library).

17. Randolph to Nicholson, December 17, 1800 (copy in Randolph Papers, Virginia State Library).

18. Randolph to Taylor, January 31, 1802 (copy in Randolph Papers, Virginia State Library).

19. *Annals of Congress* (7th Cong., 1st sess.), pp. 367–68.

20. *Ibid.* (9th Cong., 1st sess.), pp. 592–605.

21. *Ibid.*, pp. 1107–15.

22. Randolph to Nicholson, October 12, 1805 (copy in Randolph Papers, Virginia State Library).

23. See Jefferson to Monroe, May 4, 1806 (*Works of Jefferson*, XI, 106).

24. Randolph to St. George Randolph (Randolph MSS, Duke University).

25. Randolph to Key, September 12, 1813 (Hugh Garland, *Randolph of Roanoke*, II, 20).

26. *Ibid.*, p. 71.

27. *Richmond Enquirer*, April 1, 1815.

28. Randolph to Gilmer, December 27, 1821 (Richard B. Davis, *Francis Walker Gilmer*, p. 117).

29. *Annals of Congress* (17th Cong., 1st sess.), p. 820.

30. *Ibid.*, p. 933.

31. *Ibid.*, p. 936.

32. *Ibid.*, p. 944.

33. "Randolphiana," *Richmond Enquirer*, June 18, 1833.

34. *Ibid.*, June 21, 1833.

35. Notes on Randolph (Loughborough MSS, copy in Randolph Papers, Virginia State Library).

36. "Randolphiana," *Richmond Enquirer*, June 25, 1833.

37. *Annals of Congress* (18th Cong., 1st sess.), p. 1302.

38. *Ibid.*, p. 1304.

39. *Richmond Enquirer*, June 4, 1824.

40. F. J. C. Hearnshaw (ed.), *Social and Political Ideas of Some Representative Thinkers of the Revolutionary Era*, p. 93.

41. Burke, "Reflections on the Revolution in France," *Works*, II, 331–32.

42. *Register of Debates* (19th Cong., 2d sess.), II, 125–26.

43. *Ibid.*, p. 128.

44. See Fenimore Cooper, *Sketches of Switzerland*, II, 18.

45. *Richmond Enquirer*, May 25, 1824.

46. *Proceedings and Debates of the Virginia State Convention*, p. 411.

47. *Ibid.*, p. 313.

48. *Ibid.*, p. 316.

49. *Ibid.,* p. 317.
50. *Ibid.,* p. 319.
51. *Ibid.,* p. 533.
52. *Ibid.,* p. 556.
53. George Santayana, *Reason in Society,* p. 47.
54. *Proceedings and Debates of the Virginia State Convention,* p. 815.
55. *Ibid.,* p. 870.
56. Randolph to Jackson, March 1, 1832 (*Correspondence of Jackson,* IV, 413–14).
57. *Richmond Enquirer,* February 13, 1830.
58. Garland, *op. cit.,* II, 346.
59. *Ibid.,* I, 19.
60. *Ibid.,* II, 360.
61. See John Taylor, *Definition of Parties,* p. 9.
62. *Richmond Enquirer,* June 4, 1824.
63. John C. Calhoun, *Discourse on the Constitution, Works,* I, 511–12.

## CHAPTER FOUR

### THE DIVISION OF POWER

1. *Annals of Congress* (12th Cong., 2d sess.), pp. 184–85.
2. See William Cabell Bruce, *Randolph,* II, 228.
3. Notes on Randolph (Nathan Loughborough MSS, copy in Randolph Papers, Virginia State Library).
4. *Annals of Congress* (8th Cong., 2d sess.), pp. 705–6.
5. *Ibid.,* pp. 768–70.
6. Hugh Henry Brackenridge, *Modern Chivalry,* p. 17.
7. Randolph to St. George Tucker, January 15, 1801 (copy in Virginia State Library).
8. *Annals of Congress* (10th Cong., 1st sess.), p. 68.
9. *Ibid.* (17th Cong., 1st sess.), p. 903.
10. Randolph to Alexander, June 26, 1832 (Hugh Garland, *Randolph of Roanoke,* II, 353).
11. Edmund Quincy, *Life of Josiah Quincy,* p. 339.
12. John C. Calhoun, *Discourses on the Constitution, Works,* I, 300.
13. Henry Adams, *John Randolph,* p. 37.
14. Garland, *op. cit.,* II, 51–62.
15. Letter to Edward Booker, 1816 (copy in Randolph Papers, Virginia State Library); see Bruce, *op. cit.,* II, 240.
16. *Annals of Congress* (14th Cong., 1st sess.), p. 840.

17. Charles W. Wiltse, *John C. Calhoun, Nationalist,* p. 108.
18. Adams, *op. cit.,* p. 272.
19. *Annals of Congress* (14th Cong., 1st sess.), p. 844.
20. *Ibid.,* pp. 533–38.
21. *Richmond Enquirer,* January 24, 1822.
22. Leigh to Randolph, April 3, 1826 (Randolph Letters, University of North Carolina).
23. Jefferson to Macon, August 19, 1821 (Macon Papers, North Carolina Department of Archives and History).
24. *Annals of Congress* (18th Cong., 1st sess.), I, 1300.
25. *Ibid.,* p. 1303.
26. *Ibid.,* pp. 1306–7.
27. *Ibid.,* p. 1305.
28. Wilhelm Röpke, *The Social Crisis of Our Time.*
29. *Annals of Congress* (18th Cong., 1st sess.), I, 1310–11.
30. *Ibid.,* p. 1300.
31. See *Reminiscences of Benj: Perley Poore,* I, 210.
32. See Gerald M. Capers, "Reconsideration of John C. Calhoun's Transition from Nationalism to Nullification," *Journal of Southern History,* XIV, 34–48; and Wiltse, *op. cit.,* p. 289.
33. Wiltse, *op. cit.,* p. 286.
34. *Annals of Congress* (18th Cong., 1st sess.), II, 2359–60.
35. *Ibid.,* p. 2360.
36. *Ibid.,* p. 2368.
37. *Ibid.,* p. 2369.
38. *Ibid.,* p. 2376.
39. *Ibid.,* p. 2379.
40. Randolph to Brockenbrough, January 12, 1829 (Garland, *op. cit.,* II, 318).
41. *Proceedings and Debates of the Virginia State Convention,* p. 315.
42. Randolph to Brockenbrough, February 11, 1827 (Garland, *op. cit.,* II, 284).
43. *Reminiscences of Benj: Perley Poore,* I, 65.
44. Adams, *op. cit.,* p. 291.
45. Randolph to Jackson, March 28, 1832 (*Correspondence of Jackson,* IV, 420).
46. Randolph to Jackson, March 28, 1832 (*ibid.,* p. 429).
47. Beverley Tucker to James Henry Hammond, March 26, 1850 (Hammond Papers, Library of Congress).
48. Garland, *op. cit.,* II, 358.
49. *Ibid.,* p. 359.

50. Powhatan Bouldin, *Home Reminiscences of John Randolph,* p. 180.
51. *Ibid.,* p. 181.
52. Adams, *op. cit.,* p. 273.
53. Garland, *op. cit.,* II, 359.

## CHAPTER FIVE

### The Planter-Statesman

1. John Taylor, *Definition of Parties,* p. 8.
2. See Henry Adams, *History of the United States,* IV, 281.
3. *Annals of Congress* (14th Cong., 1st sess.), p. 688.
4. Randolph to Quincy, August 30, 1813 (Edmund Quincy, *Life of Josiah Quincy,* p. 336).
5. Tucker to Garnett, July 5, 1811 (Henry St. George Tucker Papers, Duke University).
6. Randolph to Brockenbrough, July 24, 1824 (Hugh Garland, *Randolph of Roanoke,* II, 225).
7. *Proceedings and Debates of the Virginia State Convention,* p. 790.
8. See Randolph to Quincy, July 1, 1824 (Edmund Quincy, *op. cit.,* p. 353).
9. Jefferson to Du Pont, June 28, 1809 (*Correspondence between Jefferson and Du Pont de Nemours,* pp. 124–27).
10. *Annals of Congress* (18th Cong., 1st sess.), I, 2362.
11. John Taylor, *Inquiry into the Principles and Policy of the United States,* p. 61.
12. *Richmond Enquirer,* April 1, 1815.
13. Randolph to Nicholson, October 15, 1803 (copy in Randolph Papers, Virginia State Library).
14. See Randolph's letter, the first of a series, signed "Decius," *Richmond Enquirer,* August 15, 1806.
15. *Annals of Congress* (18th Cong., 1st sess.), I, 1310.
16. Edmund Quincy, *op. cit.,* p. 343.
17. Macon to N. W. Edwards, February 17, 1828 (Macon Papers, North Carolina State Department of Archives and History).
18. *Proceedings and Debates of the Virginia State Convention,* p. 493.
19. *Ibid.,* p. 802.
20. Taylor to J. M. Garnett, December 17, 1807 (Garnett MSS, Duke University).
21. See esp. *Annals of Congress* (10th Cong., 1st sess.), pp. 1904–12.
22. *Richmond Enquirer,* December 5, 1812.
23. *Annals of Congress* (12th Cong., 1st sess.), pp. 442–48.

24. *Richmond Enquirer,* April 1, 1815.
25. *Annals of Congress* (14th Cong., 1st sess.), p. 845.
26. *Richmond Enquirer,* January 14, 1813.
27. *Ibid.,* January 27, 1816.
28. *Ibid.,* January 31, 1824.
29. Brockenbrough to Randolph (?), 1808 (?) (copy in Randolph Letters, University of North Carolina).
30. *Annals of Congress* (9th Cong., 1st sess.), p. 560.
31. Garland, *op. cit.,* I, 213.
32. *Annals of Congress* (14th Cong., 1st sess.), pp. 683–88.
33. *Ibid.* (18th Cong., 1st sess.), II, 2360.
34. Macon to N. W. Edwards, March 3, 1828 (Macon Papers, North Carolina State Department of Archives and History).
35. W. C. Bruce, *Randolph,* I, 430.
36. *Annals of Congress* (14th Cong., 1st sess.), pp. 1110–13.
37. *Ibid.,* p. 1339.
38. *Ibid.* (12th Cong., 1st sess.), p. 525.

## CHAPTER SIX

### The Cancer

1. See K. M. Rowland, *The Life of George Mason,* II, 161.
2. Thomas Jefferson, *Notes on the State of Virginia,* p. 237.
3. St. George Tucker, *A Dissertation on Slavery,* p. 1.
4. *Register of Debates* (24th Cong., 2d sess.), p. 2186.
5. Henry Adams, *Randolph,* p. 21; Hugh Garland, *Randolph of Roanoke,* II, 224.
6. *Register of Debates* (19th Cong., 1st sess.), p. 118.
7. Powhatan Bouldin, *Home Reminiscences of John Randolph,* p. 32.
8. Josiah Quincy, *Figures of the Past,* p. 228.
9. Randolph to Leigh, December 15, 1830 (Randolph Letters, University of North Carolina).
10. Garland, *op. cit.,* II, 222; also "Randolphiana," *Richmond Enquirer,* June 25, 1833.
11. Garland, *op. cit.,* II, 223.
12. *Ibid.,* p. 44.
13. Randolph to Leigh, September 17, 1832 (Randolph MSS, Duke University).
14. Garland, *op. cit.,* II, 150.
15. Written in 1846. See Mary H. Coleman, "Whittier on Randolph,"

*New England Quarterly*, VIII, 551–54.

16. *Annals of Congress* (6th Cong., 1st sess.), pp. 233–34.

17. *Ibid.*, p. 244.

18. Randolph to Nicholson, September 26, 1800 (copy in Randolph Papers, Virginia State Library).

19. *American State Papers*, Class VIII: *Public Lands*, I, No. 76, 160 (7th Cong., 2d sess.), "Indian Territory."

20. Randolph to Tazewell, January 8, 1804 (copy in Randolph Papers, Virginia State Library).

21. *Annals of Congress* (9th Cong., 2d sess.), p. 238.

22. *Ibid.*, p. 528.

23. *Ibid.*, p. 626.

24. *Ibid.*, p. 627.

25. Adams, *op. cit.*, chap. xi.

26. *Annals of Congress* (12th Cong., 1st sess.), I, 450–51.

27. *Ibid.* (14th Cong., 1st sess.), pp. 1115–16.

28. *Ibid.* (16th Cong., 1st sess.), pp. 925–26.

29. *Richmond Enquirer*, January 18, 1820.

30. Randolph to Rutledge, March 20, 1820 (Randolph MSS, Duke University).

31. *Congressional Globe* (25th Cong., 2d sess.), Appendix, p. 70.

32. *Annals of Congress* (16th Cong., 2d sess.), p. 1161.

33. *Ibid.* (18th Cong., 1st sess.), p. 1308.

34. *Richmond Enquirer*, January 31, 1824.

35. *Annals of Congress* (18th Cong., 1st sess.), II, 2381.

36. *Register of Debates* (19th Cong., 1st sess.), pp. 117–18.

37. *Ibid.*, pp. 130–31.

38. Randolph to Leigh, April 3, 1826 (copy in Randolph Letters, University of North Carolina).

39. Foster to Josiah Quincy, July 18, 1839 (Edmund Quincy, *Life of Josiah Quincy*, pp. 462–63).

40. *Niles' Register*, VI (3d ser.), 453.

41. Josiah Quincy, *op. cit.*, pp. 212–13.

42. *Proceedings and Debates of the Virginia State Convention*, p. 838.

43. Bouldin, *op. cit.*, pp. 189–90.

44. Randolph to William Wallace, March 17, 1832 (Randolph MSS, Duke University).

45. Randolph to Jackson, March 27, 1832 (*Correspondence of Jackson*, IV, 421–22).

46. See John Taylor, *Arator*, p. 55; *Construction Construed*, p. 301.

47. Randolph to Quincy, March 22, 1814 (Edmund Quincy, *op. cit.,* p. 351).

48. Garland, *op. cit.,* II, 59–60.

49. *Ibid.,* p. 71.

50. *Ibid.,* pp. 100–101.

51. *Ibid.,* p. 133.

52. *Ibid.,* pp. 149–50.

53. See the *Richmond Enquirer,* July 2 and July 5, 1822; also *Niles' Register,* I (2d ser.), 327.

54. Garland, *op. cit.,* II, 193.

55. *Register of Debates* (19th Cong., 1st sess.), p. 117.


CHAPTER SEVEN

CHANGE IS NOT REFORM

1. *Proceedings and Debates of the Virginia State Convention,* p. 802.

2. *Works of John Adams,* X, 226.

3. Randolph to Hay, January 6, 1806 (Randolph Letters, University of North Carolina).

4. Randolph to Quincy, March 22, 1814 (Edmund Quincy, *Life of Josiah Quincy,* p. 351).

5. *Ibid.,* pp. 353–55.

6. Randolph to James M. Garnett, February 10, 1815 (copy in Randolph Papers, Virginia State Library).

7. Hugh Garland, *Randolph of Roanoke,* II, 80–81.

8. Richard B. Davis, *Francis Walker Gilmer,* p. 176.

9. Randolph to Monroe, June 15, 1803 (copy in Randolph Papers, Virginia State Library).

10. Randolph to Tazewell, April 21, 1804 (copy in Randolph Papers, Virginia State Library).

11. Garland, *op. cit.,* II, 274.

12. Randolph to Brockenbrough (*ibid.,* p. 345).

13. *Ibid.,* p. 317.

14. *Correspondence of Jackson,* IV, 428.

15. Randolph to Brockenbrough, August 10, 1826 (Garland, *op. cit.,* II, 309).

16. Randolph to Brockenbrough, December 15, 1827 (*ibid.,* p. 295).

17. See J. W. Pratt, *Expansionists of 1812,* p. 147.

18. *Annals of Congress* (8th Cong., 1st sess.), p. 434.

19. *Ibid.* (9th Cong., 1st sess.), p. 928.

20. *Ibid.* (17th Cong., 1st sess.), p. 943.

21. Randolph to Quincy, October 18, 1813 (Quincy, *op. cit.*, p. 337).

22. Randolph to Brockenbrough, March 2, 1814 (Garland, *op. cit.*, II, 33).

23. *Annals of Congress* (16th Cong., 1st sess.), p. 942.

24. *Ibid.* (17th Cong., 1st sess.), pp. 819–22.

25. *Ibid.*, p. 942.

26. Powhatan Bouldin, *Home Reminiscences of John Randolph*, pp. 276–78.

27. See "Randolph's Grave," *Littell's Living Age*, XI, 195.

28. *Annals of Congress* (9th Cong., 1st sess.), pp. 500–502.

29. Randolph to Quincy, October 18, 1813 (Quincy, *op. cit.*, pp. 337–38).

30. *Annals of Congress* (14th Cong., 1st sess.), p. 1132.

31. *Ibid.* (17th Cong., 1st sess.), pp. 820–21.

32. *Richmond Enquirer,* June 8, 1824.

33. *Proceedings and Debates of the Virginia State Convention,* pp. 313–21.

34. *Ibid.*, p. 492.

35. *Ibid.*, pp. 789–91.

36. *Ibid.*, p. 802.

37. Randolph to William Wallace, March 17, 1832 (Randolph MSS, Duke University).

38. R. H. Gabriel, *The Course of American Democratic Thought*, p. 12.

39. Nathaniel Beverley Tucker, "An Account of John Randolph," *Historical Magazine*, III, 187–88.

40. Keith Feiling, *Sketches in Nineteenth Century Biography*, p. 39.

41. Margaret Coit, *John C. Calhoun*, p. 171.

42. John C. Calhoun, *Works*, VI, 347.

43. John S. Wise, *The End of an Era*, p. 441.

44. Calhoun, *op. cit.*, II, 649.

# A Randolph Chronology

*June 2, 1773.* John Randolph born at Cawsons, Virginia, near the mouth of the Appomattox.

*January 3, 1781.* Flight of Mrs. Tucker and her children from the British under Arnold.

*1787.* Randolph at Princeton.

*1788–89.* Randolph at Columbia College.

*1790–91.* Randolph studies law under Edmund Randolph.

*December, 1799.* Randolph enters Congress.

*December, 1801.* Randolph assumes leadership of the majority in the House of Representatives.

*January 29, 1805.* Randolph commences his denunciation of the Yazoo scandal.

*February 9, 1805.* Randolph prosecutes Justice Chase.

*December, 1805.* Randolph quarrels with Jefferson and Madison over the projected purchase of Florida from France.

*March 5, 1806.* Randolph's speech against Gregg's Resolution.

*April, 1806.* Randolph denounces the Florida negotiations and the Yazoo men and breaks with the Jeffersonians.

*May, 1807.* Randolph foreman of the grand jury in the case of Aaron Burr.

*December 10, 1811.* Randolph's speech against war with England.

*April, 1813.* Randolph loses his seat in Congress.

*April, 1815.* Randolph regains his seat in the House.

*January, 1816.* Randolph attacks the Bank of the United States. He debates with Calhoun on the revenue bill.

*February, 1820.* Randolph opposes the Missouri Compromise.

*March–November, 1822.* Randolph's first visit to England.

*January, 1824.* Randolph speaks on the Greek question and against internal improvements.

*April, 1824.* Randolph opposes the tariff of 1824.

*December 17, 1825.* Randolph elected by the Virginia legislature to the Senate.

*April, 1826.* Randolph's speech on the Panama Mission and his consequent duel with Clay.

*May–November, 1826.* Randolph's third trip abroad, to England, Holland, and France.

( 175 )

*January, 1827.* Randolph defeated for the Senate.

*April, 1827.* Randolph elected to the House of Representatives.

*1828.* Randolph supports Jackson for the presidency.

*March, 1829.* Randolph retires from Congress.

*December 30, 1829.* Randolph's speech on change at the Virginia Convention.

*May, 1830—autumn, 1831.* Randolph serves as minister to Russia.

*February, 1833.* Randolph denounces Jackson for his proclamation against South Carolina.

*May 24, 1833.* Randolph dies in Philadelphia.

# A Select Bibliography

## MANUSCRIPTS

ELLIS-MUNFORD PAPERS. Duke University Library.

JAMES M. GARNETT PAPERS. Duke University Library.

NATHANIEL MACON PAPERS. North Carolina State Department of Archives and History.

JOHN P. MATTHEWS PAPERS. Duke University.

JOHN RANDOLPH LETTERS (copies). University of North Carolina Library.

JOHN RANDOLPH PAPERS. Virginia State Library (collected by WILLIAM CABELL BRUCE).

RICHARD STANFORD PAPERS. North Carolina State Department of Archives and History.

JOHN TAYLOR PAPERS. Duke University Library.

HENRY ST. GEORGE TUCKER PAPERS. Duke University.

## NEWSPAPERS

*Niles' Weekly Register.* Various dates.

*Richmond Enquirer,* 1804–33.

*Virginia Argus,* 1800–1833.

## PRINTED DOCUMENTS

*Abridgement of the Debates of Congress.* 1797–1833. Compiled by THOMAS HART BENTON. New York, 1860.

*American State Papers,* Class VIII: *Public Lands,* Vol. I. Washington, D.C., 1833.

*Annals of Congress: Fifth Congress, First Session—Eighteenth Congress, First Session.* Washington, D.C., 1851.

*Proceedings and Debates of the Virginia State Convention of 1829–1830.* Richmond, 1830.

*Register of Debates in Congress.* 1824–37. Washington, D.C., 1825–37.

## PERIODICAL ARTICLES

ANON. "The Grave of John Randolph," *Littell's Living Age,* XIV (October, 1846), 195.

# Randolph of Roanoke

ANON. "John Randolph's Case: Dr. Parrish's Deposition," *Littell's Living Age,* XV (October, 1847), 153–56.

BOULDIN, POWHATAN. "John Randolph of Roanoke: Recollections and Unpublished Letters," *Century Magazine,* LI (March, 1896), 712–18.

CAPERS, GERALD M. "A Reconsideration of John C. Calhoun's Transition from Nationalism to Nullification," *Journal of Southern History,* Vol. XIV, No. 1 (February, 1948).

COLEMAN, MARY HALDANE. "Whittier on John Randolph of Roanoke," *New England Quarterly,* VIII (December, 1935), 551–54.

GREGORY, HORACE. "Our Writers and the Democratic Myth," *Bookman,* LXXV (August, 1932), 377–82.

GRIGSBY, HUGH BLAIR. "The Library of John Randolph," *Southern Literary Messenger,* XX (February, 1854), 79–82.

HONEYWELL, ROY J. "President Jefferson and His Successor," *American Historical Review,* XLVI (October, 1940), 64–75.

OGDEN, H. V. S. "The Decline of Lockian Political Authority in England," *American Historical Review,* XLVI (October, 1940), 21–44.

[RANDOLPH, JOHN.] "Pickings from a Portfolio of Autography: Two MS. Letters of John Randolph," *Southern Literary Messenger,* XXIII (November, 1836), 379–85.

SANFORD, WILLIAM. "John Randolph of Roanoke," *Scott's Monthly Magazine,* II (August, 1866), 624–32.

TUCKER, NATHANIEL BEVERLEY. "Account of John Randolph," *Historical Magazine,* III (June, 1859), 187–88.

———. "Correspondence of Judge Tucker," *William and Mary College Quarterly Historical Magazine,* XII (October, 1903), 84–95.

———. "Garland's Life of Randolph," *Southern Quarterly Review,* IV (new ser.; July, 1851), 41–46.

———. "Manuscripts of John Randolph," *Southern Literary Messenger,* II (July, 1836), 461–64.

## BOOKS AND PAMPHLETS

ADAMS, HENRY, *History of the United States of America during the Administrations of Jefferson and Madison.* 9 vols. New York, 1891–98.

———. *John Randolph.* Boston and New York, 1882.

———. *The Writings of Albert Gallatin.* 3 vols. Philadelphia, 1879.

ADAMS, JAMES TRUSLOW. *The Living Jefferson.* New York, 1936.

ADAMS, JOHN QUINCY. *Memoirs of John Quincy Adams.* Edited by CHARLES FRANCIS ADAMS. 12 vols. Philadelphia, 1874–77.

# A Select Bibliography

AMBLER, CHARLES HENRY. *Sectionalism in Virginia from 1776 to 1861.* Chicago, 1910.

——. *Thomas Ritchie: A Study in Virginia Politics.* Richmond, 1913.

BALDWIN, JOSEPH GLOVER. *Party Leaders.* New York, 1855.

BEARD, CHARLES A. *The Economic Origins of Jeffersonian Democracy.* New York, 1915.

——. *Jefferson, Corporations and the Constitution.* Washington, D.C., 1936.

BECKER, CARL. *The Declaration of Independence: A Study in the History of Political Ideas.* New York, 1922.

BENTON, THOMAS HART. *Thirty Years' View.* 2 vols. New York, 1854.

BEVERIDGE, ALBERT J. *The Life of John Marshall.* 4 vols. Boston, 1916.

BLAND, THEODORICK. *The Bland Papers.* Edited by CHARLES CAMPBELL. Petersburg, Va., 1840–43.

BOULDIN, POWHATAN. *Home Reminiscences of John Randolph of Roanoke.* Richmond, 1837.

BOWERS, CLAUDE. *Jefferson in Power.* New York, 1937.

BRACKENRIDGE, HUGH HENRY. *Modern Chivalry.* Edited by CLAUDE NEWLIN. New York, 1937.

BRADFORD, GAMALIEL. *Damaged Souls.* New York, 1922.

BRUCE, PHILIP A. *John Randolph.* ("Library of Southern Literature," Vol. X.) Atlanta, 1907.

——. *The Virginia Plutarch.* 2 vols. Chapel Hill, 1929.

BRUCE, WILLIAM CABELL. *Below the James.* Boston, 1937.

——. *John Randolph of Roanoke.* New York, 1922.

BURKE, EDMUND. *Works.* 8 vols. London, 1857.

BURY, J. B. *The Idea of Progress.* London, 1921.

CALHOUN, JOHN C. *Works.* Edited by R. K. CRALLÉ. 6 vols. New York, 1853–55.

CARPENTER, JESSE T. *The South as a Conscious Minority, 1789–1861.* New York, 1930.

CHANNING, EDWARD. *A History of the United States.* 6 vols. New York, 1912–32.

CHINARD, GILBERT. *Thomas Jefferson: The Apostle of Americanism.* Boston, 1928.

COBBAN, ALFRED. *Edmund Burke and the Revolt against the Eighteenth Century.* London, 1929.

COIT, MARGARET. *John C. Calhoun, American Portrait.* Boston, 1950.

COLEMAN, MARY HALDANE. *St. George Tucker, Citizen of No Mean City.* Richmond, 1938.

## Randolph of Roanoke

CONWAY, MONCURE DANIEL. *Omitted Chapters of History Disclosed in the Life and Papers of Edmund Randolph.* New York, 1888.

COOPER, JAMES FENIMORE. *The American Democrat.* Cooperstown, N.Y., 1837.

COOPER, THOMAS. *Lectures on the Elements of Political Economy.* Columbia, S.C., 1826.

CRAIGHILL, ROBERT T. *The Virginia "Peerage"; or Sketches of Virginians Distinguished in Virginia's History.* Richmond, 1880.

COTTERILL, R. S. *The Old South.* Glendale, Calif., 1936.

DABNEY, RICHARD HEATH. *John Randolph: A Character Sketch.* Chicago, 1898.

DAVIDSON, DONALD. *The Attack on Leviathan: Regionalism and Nationalism in the United States.* Chapel Hill, 1938.

DAVIS, RICHARD BEALE. *Francis Walker Gilmer: Life and Learning in Jefferson's Virginia.* Richmond, 1939.

DODD, WILLIAM E. *The Cotton Kingdom: A Chronicle of the Old South.* New Haven, 1921.

DUNLAP, O. A. "The Economic Ideas of John Taylor." Unpublished Master's thesis, Duke University, 1934.

EATON, CLEMENT. *Freedom of Thought in the Old South.* Durham, N.C., 1940.

ECKENRODE, H. J. *The Randolphs.* Indianapolis, 1946.

FEILING, KEITH, *Sketches in Nineteenth Century Biography.* London, 1930.

FITZHUGH, GEORGE. *Sociology for the South.* Richmond, 1854.

GABRIEL, RALPH HENRY. *The Course of American Democratic Thought: An Intellectual History since 1815.* New York, 1940.

GARLAND, HUGH A. *The Life of John Randolph of Roanoke.* 2 vols. New York, 1850.

GILMER, FRANCIS WALKER. *Sketches, Essays, and Translations.* Baltimore, 1828.

GREEN, FLETCHER M. *Constitutional Developments in the South Atlantic States, 1776–1860.* Chapel Hill, 1930.

GRIGSBY, HUGH BLAIR. *Discourse on the Life and Character of the Hon. Littleton Waller Tazewell.* Norfolk, 1860.

HARRIS, CICERO W. *The Sectional Struggle: First Period.* Philadelphia, 1902.

HATCHER, WILLIAM B. *Edward Livingston, Jeffersonian Republican and Jacksonian Democrat.* University, La., 1940.

HAYNE, ROBERT Y., and WEBSTER, DANIEL. *The Several Speeches Made*

( 180 )

## A Select Bibliography

during the Debate in the Senate of the United States, on Mr. Foot's Resolution . . . by General Hayne and Mr. Webster. Charleston, 1830.

HEARNSHAW, F. J. C. (ed.). The Social and Political Ideas of Some Representative Thinkers of the Revolutionary Era. London, 1931.

HESSELTINE, WILLIAM B. A History of the South, 1607–1936. New York, 1936.

HOCKETT, HOMER C. The Constitutional History of the United States. 2 vols. New York, 1939–41.

HOFFMAN, ROSS, and LEVACK, PAUL. Burke's Politics. New York, 1949.

HOLST, HERMANN EDUARD VON. The Constitutional and Political History of the United States. Chicago, 1881–92.

IRVING, PIERRE M. The Life and Letters of Washington Irving. 4 vols. New York, 1864.

JACKSON, ANDREW. The Correspondence of Andrew Jackson. Edited by JOHN SPENCER BASSETT. 7 vols. Washington, D.C., 1926–35.

JACOBS, JOHN RIPLEY. Tarnished Warrior: Major-General James Wilkinson. New York, 1938.

JEFFERSON, THOMAS. The Commonplace Book of Thomas Jefferson. Edited by GILBERT CHINARD. Baltimore, 1927.

———. The Complete Anas of Thomas Jefferson. Edited by FRANKLIN B. SAWVEL. New York, 1903.

———. Correspondence between Thomas Jefferson and Pierre Samuel du Pont de Nemours. Boston, 1910.

———. The Literary Bible of Thomas Jefferson: His Commonplace Book of Philosophers and Poets. Edited by GILBERT CHINARD. Baltimore, 1928.

———. The Living Thoughts of Thomas Jefferson. Edited by JOHN DEWEY. New York, 1940.

———. Notes on the State of Virginia. Philadelphia, 1787.

———. The Writings of Thomas Jefferson. Memorial ed. 20 vols. Washington, D.C., 1904.

JENKINS, WILLIAM SUMNER. Pro-Slavery Thought in the Old South. Chapel Hill, 1935.

JOHNSON, GERALD W. America's Silver Age: The Statecraft of Clay–Webster–Calhoun. New York, 1939.

———. Randolph of Roanoke: A Political Fantastic. New York, 1929.

KENNEDY, JOHN PENDLETON. Memoirs of the Life of William Wirt. 2 vols. Philadelphia, 1849–50.

KING, CHARLES R. The Life and Correspondence of Rufus King. 5 vols. New York, 1898.

KNAPP, SAMUEL LORENZO (IGNATIUS LOYOLA ROBERTSON, pseud.). Sketches of Public Characters. New York, 1830.

LEGARÉ, HUGH SWINTON. *The Writings of Hugh Swinton Legaré*. Charleston, 1846.

LIPSKY, GEORGE A. *John Quincy Adams: His Theory and Ideas*. New York, 1950.

LODGE, HENRY CABOT. *Daniel Webster*. Boston, 1894.

MACCUNN, JOHN. *The Political Philosophy of Burke*. London, 1913.

MADISON, JAMES. *The Writings of James Madison*. Edited by GAILLARD HUNT. 8 vols. New York, 1908.

MALONE, DUMAS. *The Public Life of Thomas Cooper, 1783–1839*. New Haven, 1926.

MEIGS, WILLIAM M. *The Life of John Caldwell Calhoun*. 2 vols. New York, 1917.

MERRIAM, CHARLES E. *A History of American Political Theories*. New York, 1920.

MONROE, JAMES. *The Writings of James Monroe*. Edited by S. M. HAMILTON. 7 vols. London, 1903.

MORSE, JOHN T., JR. *John Quincy Adams*. Boston, 1882.

————. *Thomas Jefferson*. Boston, 1883.

MUDGE, EUGENE TENBROECK. *The Social Philosophy of John Taylor of Caroline: A Study in Jeffersonian Democracy*. New York, 1939.

NAMIER, L. P. *England in the Age of the American Revolution*. London, 1930.

OSBORN, ANNIE MARION. *Rousseau and Burke: A Study of the Idea of Liberty in Eighteenth-Century Political Thought*. New York, 1940.

PARKS, JOSEPH HOWARD. *Felix Grundy, Champion of Democracy*. University, La., 1940.

PARRINGTON, VERNON L. *The Romantic Revolution in America, 1800–1860*. New York, 1927.

PARTON, JAMES. *Famous Americans of Recent Times*. Boston, 1867.

PHILLIPS, ULRICH B. *American Negro Slavery*. New York, 1918.

POORE, BENJ: PERLEY. *Perley's Reminiscences of Sixty Years in the National Metropolis*. 2 vols. Philadelphia, 1886.

PRATT, JULIUS W. *The Expansionists of 1812*. New York, 1925.

QUINCY, EDMUND. *Life of Josiah Quincy of Massachusetts*. Boston, 1867.

QUINCY, JOSIAH. *Figures of the Past*. Boston, 1901.

RANDALL, HENRY STEPHENS. *The Life of Thomas Jefferson*. 3 vols. New York, 1858.

RANDOLPH, JOHN. *Letters of John Randolph to a Young Relative: Embracing a Series of Years, from Early Youth, to Mature Manhood*. Edited by THEODORE DUDLEY. Philadelphia, 1834.

RAVENEL, MRS. ST. JULIEN. *Life and Times of William Lowndes, of South Carolina, 1782–1822*. Boston, 1901.

# A Select Bibliography

RÖPKE, WILHELM. *The Social Crisis of Our Time*. Chicago, 1950.

ROUSSEAU, JEAN-JACQUES. *The Political Writings of Jean-Jacques Rousseau*. Edited by C. E. VAUGHAN. 2 vols. London, 1915.

ROWLAND, KATE MASON. *The Life of George Mason, 1724–1792*. 2 vols. New York, 1892.

RUSH, RICHARD. *John Randolph at Home and Abroad*. Philadelphia, 1828.

SANTAYANA, GEORGE. *Reason in Society*. New York, 1905.

SAWYER, LEMUEL. *A Biography of John Randolph of Roanoke*. New York, 1844.

SIMMS, HENRY HARRISON. *John Taylor of Caroline: The Story of a Brilliant Leader in the Early Virginia State Rights School*. Richmond, 1932.

SYDNOR, CHARLES S. *The Development of Southern Sectionalism, 1819–1848*. University, La., 1948.

TAYLOR, JOHN. *Arator*. Georgetown, S.C., 1814.

————. *Construction Construed, and Constitutions Vindicated*. Richmond, 1820.

————. *Definition of Parties*. Philadelphia, 1794.

————. *An Inquiry into the Principles and Policy of the Government of the United States*. Washington, D.C., 1823.

THOMAS, E. S. *Reminiscences of the Last Sixty-five Years, Commencing with the Battle of Lexington*. Hartford, 1840.

THOMAS, F. W. *John Randolph of Roanoke, and Other Sketches of Character, Including William Wirt*. Philadelphia, 1843.

TOCQUEVILLE, ALEXIS DE. *Democracy in America*. 2 vols. Edited by PHILLIPS BRADLEY. New York, 1948.

TRENT, WILLIAM P. *Southern Statesmen of the Old Regime*. New York, 1897.

TUCKER, GEORGE. *The Life of Thomas Jefferson*. 2 vols. London, 1837.

TUCKER, ST. GEORGE. *A Dissertation on Slavery*. Philadelphia, 1796.

TURNER, FREDERICK JACKSON. *The Significance of Sections in American History*. New York, 1932.

TYLER, LYON G. *The Letters and Times of the Tylers*. 2 vols. Richmond, 1884.

WILTSE, CHARLES MAURICE. *The Jeffersonian Tradition in American Democracy*. Chapel Hill, 1935.

————. *John C. Calhoun, Nationalist*. Indianapolis, 1944.

————. *John C. Calhoun, Nullifier*. Indianapolis, 1949.

WISE, JOHN S. *The End of an Era*. Boston and New York, 1899.

WOODFIN, MAUDE H. "Contemporary Opinion in Virginia of Thomas Jefferson," in *Essays in Honor of William E. Dodd*. Edited by AVERY CRAVEN. Chicago, 1935.

# Index

# Index